"My relationship with my own m..... ... it easier for me to fall in love with Mary, the mother of Jesus. That's because I saw in Mom so many of the virtues of our Blessed Mother. In these pages, these Marian virtues will come to life for you, and before you know it, you will be letting Mary spiritually mother you."

Cardinal Timothy Dolan
Archbishop of New York

"Lovely and relevant—*Imitating Mary* is food for the mother's soul! Marge Fenelon unpacks Mary's virtuous role in scripture and Church tradition and brilliantly puts it in language that modern-day mothers can identify with and readily apply to their lives. Simply beautiful!"

Donna-Marie Cooper O'Boyle
Author of *Rooted in Love*

"*Imitating Mary* is a book for mothers, but I, a man and a Jesuit priest, loved it. Through its personal stories, imaginative Gospel scenes, and reflection questions I came to better understand the vocation of motherhood and to enter more deeply into Mary's heart."

Rev. James Kubicki, S.J.
Author of *A Heart on Fire*

"So often we look to Mary as a prayerful companion but gloss over the very real fact that she was a mother who knew all the joys and struggles of raising a child. Marge Fenelon, in her beautiful book *Imitating Mary*, invites us to experience our moments of motherhood through the prism of our Blessed Mother's life."

Mary DeTurris Poust
Author of *Cravings*

"*Imitating Mary* is THE Mary book moms of all stripes have been waiting for, though they might not have known it. Fenelon makes the Blessed Mother into a real person without subtracting any of her amazing qualities. You'll want to read it, reread it, and share it with every mom you know."

Sarah A. Reinhard
Author of *A Catholic Mother's Companion to Pregnancy*

"We get so used to thinking of Mary as 'Blessed Virgin' or 'Queen of Heaven' or 'Mother of God,' we sometimes forget that she was also a real-life, flesh-and-blood mother of a real-life, flesh-and-blood child. In her latest book, Marge Fenelon vividly brings to life the Mary who had to tell Joseph she was pregnant; who faced scorn for being an unwed mother; who had to watch her son grow up, enter into his own life, and eventually die before her eyes. If you've ever had trouble relating to the Mary of icons and holy cards, *Imitating Mary* will give you insightful—and very practical—ways to allow Mary to help you become the best parent you can be."

Woodeene Koenig-Bricker
Author of *365 Mary*

Imitating *Mary*

Ten Marian Virtues
for the
MODERN MOM

Marge Fenelon

Foreword by Lisa M. Hendey

ave maria press AMP notre dame, indiana

Founded in 1865, Ave Maria Press is a ministry of the United States Province of Holy Cross.

www.avemariapress.com

Paperback: ISBN-10 1-59471-364-2, ISBN-13 978-1-59471-364-4

E-book: ISBN-10 1-59471-365-0, ISBN-13 978-1-59471-365-1

Cover image "Madonna and Child Folk Art Icon" © 2012 by Eva Campbell, www.evitaworks.com.

Cover and text design by Katherine Robinson.

Printed and bound in the United States of America.

Library of Congress Cataloging-in-Publication Data

Fenelon, Marge.

  Imitating Mary : Eight Marian Virtues for the Modern Mom / Marge Fenelon.

      pages cm

  Includes bibliographical references.

  ISBN 978-1-59471-364-4 (pbk.) -- ISBN 1-59471-364-2 (pbk.)

  1. Mary, Blessed Virgin, Saint. 2. Motherhood--Religious aspects--Catholic Church. 3. Mothers--Religious life. 4. Christian women--Religious life. I. Title.

  BT603.F46 2013

  232.91--dc23

                    2012045743

To Fr. Jonathan Niehaus, I.S.P. (1960–2012),

dear family friend, patient mentor,

and outstanding spiritual director.

Fr. Jonathan, you are greatly missed.

I can only hope to live up to what you taught me

through your words and example.

Contents

Foreword

It was completely on a whim that I registered CatholicMom. com in 2000. As the mother of two young sons, married to Greg, the love of my life (then a non-Catholic), I recall feeling completely overwhelmed not only by my motherly and spousal duties, but especially by the responsibility of raising our children in the Catholic faith.

So my motivations for buying a "dummies" computer book and starting a small website were largely selfish: I was desperate for support, encouragement, and information relevant to my vocation as a mother, especially a Catholic mother. This uniquely human desire to relate and to be in communion with one another never ceases to amaze me. Today I count most of the women with whom I connected back in those early days as dear friends. Many of them have gone on to become contributors to CatholicMom.com—a resource that welcomes hundreds of thousands of women from close to two hundred countries around the globe into a daily dialogue about the things that matter most in our lives. Together we have watched our babies be born and our children grow; we have prayed with and for one another; and we have done our very best to mentor the new moms who have come into our ever-blossoming fold.

These many years later, I still wake up each day and head anxiously to my desk with a joy for this mission that has become my life's work. While the ways in which our Church reaches out to us have developed and diversified over the centuries, its message remains as timeless as always. Although Catholic parents may have new trials and possibilities to face that are born of an ever-advancing technological culture, many of the fears, questions, delights, and joys we hold in our hearts are the same ones faced by our parents and grandparents.

As wives and single women, as stay-at-home moms and nine-to-fivers, as mothers and grandmothers, and especially as Catholics and women of faith, we are on a mission: to know, love, and serve God, to share his loving care with our family and friends, and to enjoy life with him forever in heaven. These are lofty goals that require a daily recommitment! This mission demands of us our very best. And to be at our best, we need all the help, support, and encouragement we can find.

That is why I am thrilled to join forces with my friends and colleagues at Ave Maria Press to create the CatholicMom.com Book series to support you in your life's mission. We aim to educate, uplift, and inspire you with resources that are engaging and authentically Catholic. It's our great hope that these books, complemented by what we offer at CatholicMom.com, will nurture your heart, mind, body, and soul by addressing the cares that make motherhood more than a mere status and recognize it as the vocation it is.

In *Imitating Mary* you'll find the tools to help you do that very thing—embrace your motherhood by coming to know Mary in a more intimate way. When I reflect on my own history with our Blessed Mother, it's clear to me that I didn't fully appreciate her until after I became a mother myself. In my childhood, she was my "go to" intercessor—the recipient of my laundry list of prayer intentions, since I trusted her to carry them to her son, Jesus Christ. My deepening attachment to Mary only truly began in my college years at the University of Notre Dame where I began to contemplate the nature of her Magnificat, and she became a spiritual companion to me in my daily life as a student. Still, my truest devotion to this mother of us all only came to full fruition when I first felt the complete commitment I have to my own sons. Only then could I finally begin to grasp the depth of the love this simple young woman must have held in her heart.

Mary's fiat, her "yes," her willingness to give her entire being over so fully to God's plan—with all of its glories and miseries—still continues to astonish me. As a mom, I am convinced that in an instant, without hesitation, I would lay down my life for my children. We know Mary as a witness to and a major advocate in the life and public ministry of Christ. And yet those many moments when she surely had to stand by with the deepest desire to protect her son—when she pondered in her heart and prayed fervently for all that was unfolding in their lives—point me to a grace that defies explanation and that underscores her true mission.

Because *Imitating Mary* delves into these very moments in a way that helps us understand Mary's emotions, fears, and thoughts, it becomes easy to connect with her and develop a friendship with the Mother who wants to help us embrace our vocation as mothers and daughters of God. With Mary as companion and role model, may we each know the power of our own motherly "yes" to God's perfect will for our lives, our precious families, and our world.

Lisa M. Hendey

Introduction

This book began the way all good ideas do—through a good conversation with someone I admire. A few years ago, I was talking with a young woman who confided that she was afraid to have children because she had yet to experience good mothering. She assumed that if her mother had fallen short, she would too. I did my best in the course of our chat to change her mind, but I realized quickly it would take more than a conversation.

Since that conversation, I've realized this case of self-doubt isn't an isolated one. In fact, I've observed quite a few women being tossed to and fro by a culture that's trying to convince them that motherhood is either a commodity or an affliction. It only follows that if our culture doesn't value motherhood, then it won't value the mother either. The result is the plethora of women giving up on mothering because they have no one to encourage them. Sometimes the lack of support ends in a mother becoming so stressed and overwhelmed, she turns abusive. These women aren't bad moms; they are moms who have been badly served by a culture that isn't giving them the support they need.

Then there are the mothers who are doing a great job, but they don't know it, because no one ever tells them—at least not as adamantly and frequently as moms need to hear it. They want to be perfect but don't realize their imperfections make them all the more loveable. They want the best for their kids but don't understand the best they can give is themselves. They focus on what they can't do rather than what they can do, and they haven't learned to give themselves a well-deserved pat on the back.

For all of these types of moms, I propose the same solution: Mary. In fact, she's the answer for all moms. Most of us don't realize that, with God's grace and Mary's example, we can overcome any obstacles to becoming the loving, wonderful mothers we're meant to be. In Mary, we have a mother worthy of emulation, but who is fully human with the same experiences and emotions we have. In her life, we find example, and in her virtue, we find inspiration. Mary can show us how to be the mothers we want to be—the mothers we *can* be.

In the book you're holding, you'll find an examination of Mary's life that lends itself to the modern mother. We'll look at Mary's life through ten events, or climaxes. As we do so, we'll come to know a woman who understands the frustrations of childbearing, serving her husband, loving her family, and worshipping God. In essence, we will get to know the human side of Mary. Once we've observed Mary, we'll encounter her by identifying the key virtues she practiced throughout her life, and then we'll discuss how we as mothers can live these virtues today. To facilitate our falling in love with Mary, each chapter concludes with words of wisdom to ponder, questions for personal reflection or group discussion, and a checklist of items and applications to work on until the next chapter.

My prayer is that by entrusting our motherhood to Mary, we'll become the mothers God intends for us to be, the mothers our children need, and the mothers society lacks. In that way, we can change the world, one mom at a time.

Mary's Fiat

Imitating Mary's Yes

Try to imagine for a second how today's culture would respond to something like Mary's yes to the angel Gabriel when he came to ask if Mary would bear the Son of God. Would Mary update her Facebook status? Would Gabriel be tweeting the play-by-play? Would the tabloids be filled with dramatic photos of Mary and Gabriel? Or, would the blogosphere be silent, the news networks oblivious? Whatever the case, you can be sure the reaction would be disproportional to the event, since the Annunciation is an event that changed the course of history forever.

On the day the Virgin of Nazareth gave her consent to becoming the Mother of God, a cry of jubilation rose in heaven, on earth, and under the earth. Only at that moment, with Mary's agreement, could the mystery of the Incarnation be realized. By offering her free decision, the Blessed Virgin offered the Son of God the maternal seed of life that made it possible for the Almighty to enter his creation. The Word was made flesh. A young Jewish girl agreed to the angel Gabriel's request, and God's plan for our salvation was secured. At the moment of the Annunciation, Mary set off a chain of events with far-reaching implications.

The Meaning of Mary's Fiat for Us as Christians

When Mary said yes to God's will—her fiat—our Lord was conceived in her womb. Allowing herself to become the instrument for Jesus' Incarnation also meant becoming the instrument for God's plan of salvation for us. If the Son of God didn't become man, live, preach, suffer, and die in atonement for our sins, the gates of heaven couldn't be opened to us. Mary's becoming Mother of Christ also meant her becoming Mother of his Church, and thereby fulfilling the duties that accompany that position: to nourish and educate the People of God. All of the privileges and responsibilities given to Mary in her divine motherhood also are given to her as Mother of mankind. "The Son whom she brought forth is He whom God placed as the first-born among many brethren, namely the faithful, in whose birth and education she cooperates with a maternal love," the Church tells us in the Vatican II document *Lumen Gentium*[1]. By her perpetual virginity, Mary gave up the possibility of having physical descendants in order to become spiritual Mother of the entire Church through her Son, Jesus.

Mary's universal motherhood guarantees her position as mediator and her ability to know everything about us, including our personal needs and concerns. It's generally assumed that, because of their beatific vision, the blessed in heaven see in God a mirror image, so to speak, of whatever is of personal interest to them and their mission. For example, they're able to see what happens to their relatives and to know the intentions of the persons they care about. Of course, because of her closeness to our Lord and her role in the salvific plan, this applies to Mary even more so. She knows all of our wants and needs and has great "power" to intercede for and care for us with her tender motherly love. The fact that she was conceived without original sin and remained sinless throughout her life enables her to fulfill her task of giving and nourishing the life of grace in a sinful humanity. Because she was taken up body and soul into heaven, she's capable of caring for her children in every aspect of our lives.

Next, we as individual Christians become children of Mary at the moment of our Baptism; when we become part of Christ the Head of the Church, we become part of Mary the Heart of the Church. We receive spiritual nourishment and education as our life of grace develops, and we are invited into an intimate relationship with Mary, through which we experience her inexhaustible richness as *our* Mother. Her yes to being our Lord's Mother was also her yes to being our Mother in a collective way as Church, but more notably in a singular way as uniquely cherished children.

The Meaning of Mary's Fiat for Us as Mothers

Furthermore, Mary's fiat holds particular significance for us as mothers. Not only was it her yes to being our Mother in the order of grace, but also it was her yes to showing us the way in our own motherhood. By agreeing to become the Mother of God, she agreed to become the ultimate example of genuine motherhood and to assist us in becoming genuine mothers, too. Mary lived a holy motherhood, and she wants us to live a holy motherhood so that, through our vocation as nurturers, educators, and spiritual guides of our families, we can effectively help to build the kingdom of God.

In Mary's fiat we can see the depth of her love for God and her willingness to follow his will regardless of the cost. The Savior would redeem Israel. How that would come about, Mary didn't know for certain, but she did know that being his Mother wouldn't be a stroll through the meadow. The land of the People of God was under Roman occupation; they were persecuted, oppressed, wanting, and helpless. They yearned for a champion to fulfill the promise of scripture: "The days are coming—oracle of the LORD—when I will fulfill the promise I made to the house of Israel and the house of Judah" (Jer 33:14); and "I will rescue you from the hand of the wicked, and ransom you from the power of the violent" (Jer 15:21). The people of Israel believed that God would send a redeemer to save them from their affliction. Whether the Redeemer's victory would be won physically through rebellion or spiritually through conversion, no one knew. Regardless, it would require much from Mary as his Mother.

Perhaps she could have been a trifle nervous. Although Mary had unparalleled faith, she also was completely human and subject to the same emotions as other humans beings. Don't we all at least get the jitters when given a huge responsibility?

I remember the day I found out I was pregnant with our first child. I kind of *knew* I was pregnant, but at that time, home pregnancy tests weren't reliable and the only way to know for certain was to go to the doctor. Sitting in the reception room awaiting the test results, I was absolutely elated. I knew that motherhood was in God's plan for me, and if I was pregnant, I would welcome the child with a joyous heart. On the other hand, I was scared stiff. Trailing my older siblings by several years, and being the youngest of most of the cousins, I wasn't around small children much while growing up. How would I know how to take care of a little one? For as much as I wanted a child, I was afraid of the responsibility.

I heard the receptionist call my name, and I swallowed hard. My knees wobbled as I made my way up to the desk. I breathed in deeply and let it out slowly, deliberately.

"I'm Margaret Fenelon," I said meekly.

"Your pregnancy test was positive. Congratulations, you're pregnant," the lady behind the desk said.

I was shocked, overjoyed, and terrified, all rolled into one. "Holy mackerel!" I shouted. Okay, I actually shouted holy something else, but that's beside the point. The old lady snoozing in her chair jolted upright and stared at me with big, questioning eyes. The little girl playing with the wooden alphabet puzzle at the kids' table moved over and grabbed her mom's skirt hem. The middle-aged gentleman leaned forward and examined me over the top of his newspaper. The receptionist's jaw dropped nearly to the floor.

"Um . . . that's okay, isn't it?" she asked, concerned. I suppose they didn't get many reactions like mine.

"You bet it is!" I blurted out. "Yes, it is! Oh! My goodness! I've got to go tell my husband!" I ran out of the clinic, all heads turned in my direction, wide eyes on me the whole way. I flittered across the parking lot, jumped into our car, and drove frantically home, rehearsing over and over the words I'd say to Mark to announce the conception of our firstborn.

I can't imagine Mary had the frantic reaction I had, but I bet that, upon conceiving our Lord in her womb, she felt the weight of the responsibility. She probably felt that initial "Oh! My goodness!" as I did when I found out I'd conceived my firstborn. I can even guess she paused to consider how she'd handle not only motherhood, but also divine mother-hood. Could it be that her words to the angel Gabriel, "How can this be, since I have no relations with a man?" (Lk 1:34), had more behind it than the fact she was a virgin? In addition to her virginity, she was an unwed mother, had never been a mother before, and the child she was to bear wasn't just any child; he was to be the God-Man. How's that for daunting responsibility?

Yet Mary accepted the angel's proposal without hesitation because she wanted God's will to be fulfilled in her life—and consequently our lives—more than anything else. She didn't ask for time to think about it, she didn't suggest that someone else take her place, and she certainly didn't say no! This sets precedent for us as mothers, especially if we want to follow in Mary's footsteps, figuratively speaking. Mary wanted God's will above all things, and so should we.

Saying Our Own Fiat

One of the first steps to becoming a mother like Mary is to adopt her same attitude toward our mutual Father. Based on the way Mary responded to the Holy Spirit, it seems pretty clear she had a very strong bond with God already in place.

This bond came with a certain level of understanding that she could rely on God to want what is best for her. Yet Mary likely struggled with the same trepidations that you or I would if an angel appeared to us and asked us to bear the Son of God. Just like you and I do, Mary had a vision for her future. She was probably giddy at the idea of becoming Joseph's wife and sharing a home and life with him. She likely imagined raising children to love and serve God. Surely she dreamed of growing old with her husband.

And yet she had to give up all of this when she said yes to God's will. When she became God's handmaid, she *surrendered* the plans she had for herself in lieu of the agenda given by her creator. Can you imagine forgoing all the plans you have made for your life in just a moment's time? Can you picture yourself giving up the idea of a dream wedding, a picture perfect birth, and a joy-filled adventure with your husband? It wouldn't be easy, would it?

In my experience, the first step to *letting go* as Mary modeled so beautifully with her fiat is to trust God. Trust, as you probably know, only comes with time and knowledge of oneself and he who is to be trusted. So if you find yourself anxious about turning everything over to God, know this much: First, be patient with yourself. These things take time. Second, you are not alone. Mary struggled too. Third, the more you come to know your Father, the more you will love and trust him. Lastly, when you love and trust Jesus, surrendering your life to him will come more naturally.

Try not to be discouraged if you find yourself scared in the beginning. These are uncharted territories for you and your relationship with God, and it's normal to be afraid of the unknown; but rest assured that he who is all-knowing is waiting for you to come to him, to trust him with your greatest desires and deepest fears. And when you find yourself unable to pray the prayer, "let your will be done," try starting with something a little simpler like, "give me the grace to desire your will."

Motherhood as a Vocation

If you're reading this book, it's likely that you've already accepted the idea that God's will is for you to be a mother of some sort. Maybe you have given birth to one or many children. Perhaps you're pregnant with your first. You could even be an adoptive or spiritual mother, in which case you have many souls you pray for and nurture. Whatever your circumstances, God has given you a gift in being a mother. It may not always feel like a gift (especially when your house is a wreck, no one is listening to you, and your task list seems endless), but part of the beauty of Christianity is the idea that suffering is a doorway to grace. Such is the life of a mother sometimes, and such was certainly the life of Mary.

In this way, motherhood is a vocation. It is a unique calling from God that sets us on the path to union with Christ. Sometimes it doesn't feel like a calling though. And for some women, maternity doesn't seem to suit them. They don't feel like they are fit to be mothers, and they don't feel any sort of inclination toward nurturing. On the other hand, there are many women who feel a strong yearning to bear children and a natural proclivity for mothering, yet their bodies are unable to sustain a pregnancy.

For both types of mothers, there is eternal hope in Christ and a perfect model in his mother, Mary. Physical mothers who find themselves lacking the warm feelings associated with maternity, can ask Jesus to help them be patient with themselves. They can ask him to show them how the feelings that they do have can bring joy to their family. Women who long to bear children can try their talents on children who need a strong mother figure in their life. They can consider taking on their parish priest as a "spiritual son." Above all, we should all trust that God has a plan for our lives, and that whatever that plan may be, it is indeed a gift.

Renewing Our Fiat

We can't say our fiat once; we have to say it over and over again. We need to renew it daily at the least, and optimally in every circumstance that arises in which we perceive God's request for us to consent to his will. Isn't that every moment of every day? Consider identifying certain triggers in your day to help you remember to say your yes to God. Maybe turning on your coffeemaker every morning serves as a trigger. Or, perhaps it's the sound of your car engine starting every morning before you pull out of your driveway and begin your day.

The more often we renew our fiats, the more "real" they'll become to us. When we renew them often, we learn to recognize and become more accustomed to them. Eventually, they will become like exhaling, a normal part of who we are and how we respond to the world around us. We'll grow into them, and we'll become more and more like Mary along the way. Below is a beautiful prayer I think will help us in our fiat renewal.

O Full of Grace

O Mary, "full of grace and blessed among women," stretch out the hand of your motherly protection, we ask you, upon us who gather round your queenly throne as your handmaidens, obedient to your command and resolved with your help to bring to realization in ourselves and our sisters the ideals of truth and Christian perfection.

Our eyes are fixed on you in admiration, immaculate Virgin; you who are loved by the Heavenly Father above all others! O Virgin Spouse of the Holy Spirit! Tender Mother of Jesus! Obtain for us from your Divine Son the grace to reflect your sublime virtues in our conduct, according to our age and condition of life.

Grant that we may be spotless and pure in our thoughts and in our behavior; gentle, affectionate, and sympathetic companions to our husbands; to our children solicitous, vigilant, and wise mothers; prudent administrators of our homes; exemplary citizens of our dear country; faithful daughters of the Church, ever ready to allow ourselves to be guided by her in thought and deed.

Help us, loving Mother, to be truly devoted to the duties of our state of life; help us make our homes true centers of spiritual life and active charity, schools where consciences will be rightly formed, gardens where every virtue will flourish. Give us your help that in social and political life we may be patterns of deep faith, of consistent and gracious Christian practice, of incorruptible integrity, and of well-balanced judgment based upon the solid principles of religion.

Bless these our resolutions which you have inspired us to make and the trials you have helped us to bear; may we with your aid come to see their abundant fruits in time and in eternity. Amen.

~Pope Pius XII, May 26, 1957

Enriching Our Motherhood

....

Thoughts to Ponder

Embracing God's salvific will with a full heart and impeded by no sin, she [Mary] devoted herself totally as a handmaid of the Lord to the person and work of her Son, under Him and with Him, by the grace of almighty God, serving the mystery of redemption. Rightly therefore the holy Fathers see her as used by God not merely in a passive way, but as freely cooperating in the work of human salvation through faith and obedience.

~Pope Paul VI, *Lumen Gentium,* November 21, 1964, 56

Deepening Our Motherhood

....

Reflection and Application

- What does motherhood mean to you?

- Recall the day you learned you were pregnant with your firstborn. If you're an adoptive or foster mother, recall the day you received your first child. What went through your mind and heart? Why?

- What might hold you back from speaking your own fiat to God's will in your life, particularly in regard to your motherhood?

- Imagine you've been approached by God's messenger as Mary was. What does your fiat sound like? What will you say to him?

Becoming a Woman of the Fiat

Imitating Mary's Yes

1. Consider what Mary's fiat means for you as a Christian.

2. Consider what Mary's fiat means for you as a mother.

3. Recognize that motherhood is a vocation.

4. Create "triggers" in your day to help you say your own fiat.

5. Ask Mary to help you to become a woman of the fiat.

Chapter 2

The Unwed
Mother

Imitating Mary's Patience

Marriage Customs in Mary's Time

In Israel during Mary's time, young couples entered into marriages arranged by their families and negotiated by the fathers or between the bride's father and her future husband. It's possible that in Galilee mothers had input into their daughters' marriage arrangements, and widows may have taken a more active role in their own remarriages. Roman law set the minimum age of marriage for girls at twelve and for boys at fourteen. This meant that marriage for girls usually took place between the ages of twelve and thirteen, which allowed for a maximum number of childbearing years and a guarantee of virginity before marriage.[1]

Additionally, the Jewish custom of marriage included two stages. The first stage was the betrothal, which was a formal exchange of the couple's consent to marry before witnesses and accompanied by a payment from the bride's family to the groom. The betrothal was legally binding, yet the girl continued to live in her family home. At this point, the couple was considered husband and wife, and the man had legal rights over the woman; any sexual relations outside of this union were considered adulterous. After one year, the couple entered the second stage of marriage, in which the young woman moved from her family home into her husband's family home during a special ceremony. At this point, the couple could exercise their full marital rights.[2]

According to the gospels of both Matthew and Luke, Mary's pregnancy took place after the betrothal, but before the completion of the marriage custom. Therefore, it seemed apparent that Mary had committed adultery, since Joseph knew that the child was not his. If convicted of adultery, Mary could have been stoned to death. Rather than risk Mary's reputation—and perhaps even her life—Joseph decided not to progress to the second stage of the marriage ritual (thus divorcing Mary) without making a fuss.

Joseph's Justice

> Now this is how the birth of Jesus Christ came about. When his mother Mary had been betrothed to Joseph, but before they lived together, she was found with child through the holy Spirit. Joseph her husband, since he was a righteous man, yet unwilling to expose her to shame, decided to divorce her quietly.
>
> Matthew 1:18–19

In the passage above, the words "righteous" and "unwilling" catch my attention. The evangelist called Joseph a righteous man—a meaningful term. A person who is righteous is just and is guided by truth, reason, and fairness. A just person is someone who weighs things carefully and tries to find solutions that are kind and equitable. Joseph wanted to be just to Mary; he wanted what was best for her even though, as far as he understood, she had cheated on him.

The second word, "unwilling," provides insight into Mary and Joseph's relationship. If he was unwilling to shame her, then they must have truly loved each other. If it were merely a marriage arranged for convenience or family tradition, wouldn't Joseph have had an easier time letting go? Clearly, he was not acting out of vengeance, but rather with pain and sorrow at the realization that his beloved was not the woman he thought she was (this was before the angel appeared to Joseph explaining the child's true identity). No, Joseph didn't want to ruin Mary's reputation or harm her in any way. I wonder if, by divorcing her quietly, he was hoping to open a door for her to safely reconstruct her life in order to care for her child unprovoked. How Joseph must have agonized over his decision!

Have you ever had to make a decision like that? Perhaps it would affect someone's reputation, or cause unfortunate consequences. Maybe it was neither, but it was hard to make for other reasons. Or, you could have been the one on the receiving end of the decision. Thinking back to that time will give you a small taste of what Joseph and Mary went through during their betrothal.

Mary's Heartache

What about the heartache that Mary likely felt? She was pregnant, and it wasn't the child of the man she was in the process of marrying. Yet she had not violated the marriage contract. What's more, the child within her womb wasn't just any child—he was the Son of God! That goes far beyond any human reason. On top of all this, Mary alone knew the truth; she had no way to prove what had happened. How would she explain to Joseph that she had not been unfaithful? How could she assure him of her ardent love and unending devotion? How could she make him believe that she still was the pure, noble woman to whom he was betrothed? How could she explain to Joseph whom she had conceived and how? How impossible it must have seemed for her to help Joseph believe a seemingly crazy story about an angel named Gabriel appearing to her and announcing to her that the heavenly Father wanted her participation in his divine plan. It was going to take some finesse and a lot of patience.

Knowing how much Joseph and Mary loved each other, I would assume Mary wanted to be the one to tell Joseph she was pregnant. Hearing it from someone else would have been a crushing blow. Mary was truthful and good; she probably wanted to handle the moment herself so as to spare Joseph any more pain or shame than he would already experience finding out from her. We can only imagine the conversation between Mary and Joseph when Mary informed him of her pregnancy. Perhaps they took a quiet walk together along the foothills of Mount Tabor or through the flora along a wildflower-lined stream. Or, maybe it was better to patiently sit by his side as he worked on a chair or table so that she wouldn't have to see the intensity of the agony in his eyes. The gentle rhythm of his carpenter's tools may have calmed and comforted her, reminding her that God was at work on Joseph's heart just as Joseph's hands were at work on the wood. How many times did she rehearse the conversation in her mind before she approached him? No doubt she prayed at length, asking God's grace and guidance for herself and an open heart and mind for her betrothed. If we could place Mary and Joseph into a modern setting and be a fly on the wall during their conversation about Mary's pregnancy, we might find ourselves hearing something like this:

"Honey, I have something very important to tell you, something you might have a hard time understanding. But, before I tell you, I want to assure you of my absolute love and fidelity.

"No, I didn't break the heirloom water jar from your parents. It's something a little harder to understand than that.

"Just come right out and say it? Okay, but first can you tell me again how much you love me?

"Stalling? Well, kind of. This isn't so easy to say. But, here goes. I'm pregnant.

"Yes, I'm sure.

"No, honest, it's not another guy.

"Explain? Well, uh . . . there was this angel. He told me his name was Gabriel and that God wanted me to be the Mother of his Son.

"Joking? No, I'm not joking—honest.

"How did the baby get there? Good question. Well, it just kind of . . . was there. I started feeling the life inside of me.

"Now what? Um . . . I was hoping that was something you could tell me."

Exploring the scene in this way really drives home how difficult it must have been for both Joseph and Mary to come to terms with Mary's pregnancy.

Modeling Mary and Joseph

Think of the last time you had a misunderstanding with someone you love. Do you remember how difficult it was to wait for him to be able to understand your perspective? Perhaps you had an argument, made a terrible mistake, your intentions were misread, or you were accused of doing something of which you were innocent. Maybe there was a major decision to make or problem to be solved, and you weren't able to communicate your thoughts and feelings—or the other was unable to communicate his thoughts and feelings to you. These are all dilemmas similar to the one Mary faced in revealing her pregnancy to Joseph, and she surely felt the same heart-wrenching, head-throbbing, gut-churning emotions as you did.

Considering how Mary so patiently handled her situation with Joseph can help you in handling similar situations in your own life. It doesn't say directly in scripture, but I can imagine that Mary sensed a need to allow Joseph space to sort it through. She had no way to prove that she had not committed adultery, and no way to assure Joseph that she'd conceived through the power of the Holy Spirit and not by another man. She'd have to wait for God to reveal this to Joseph, redeem her reputation, and restore their relationship.

Sometimes that's all you can do, too. You try to set things right, to bridge the gap, to prove yourself, or to allow others to prove themselves, but it seems like it's no use. The harder you try, the worse things get. Or, perhaps nobody has the energy to try anymore, and things start to fall apart. Those are the times when, like Mary, you give others space to sort it through on their own and allow God to reveal the truth—to them, and to you.

When the difficulty involves your spouse, you can spiral into a state of confusion and loneliness. It can seem like things will never be right again. You can feel unsure of yourself and of your relationship. It's hard to wait for things to work out because you depend on your spouse, and when something divides the two of you—even a small argument—it can leave you feeling helpless, alone, and unable to carry out even basic daily tasks. The last thing you want is to wait for God to reveal the truth; you'd rather just jump in and fix it yourself. Now.

When the difficulty involves your children, it can be downright distressing. As a mother, you're bound to set things right for your children and to guide them in every step. Because you're older and more mature, you're supposed to have a handle on it, right? But that's not always the case. Sometimes

you can't communicate well, can't understand where your
child is coming from, or are misinterpreting words and actions.
Sometimes children need to rebel, either because it's part of
their temperament or because they're testing their independence. Either way, it can be very painful. While usually you're
able to teach, nurture, and encourage your children, there also
are times when you're unable to get through to them for one
reason or another and need to step back a little in order to let
them figure things out. You never want to allow them to enter
any moral or physical danger, and if that's the case, you need
to speak up or take necessary action. In most cases, however,
you need to follow the example of Mary's patience and allow
God to work on the other's heart in his own way and timing.

Standing Back

When our oldest son, Matthew, was about twelve months old,
he decided he was going to learn to walk. I really mean *he*
decided! After breakfast one day, I set him down on the living room floor with some toys to play. He didn't want to play.
Instead, he crawled over to the couch, pulled himself up to a
standing position, turned around, and tried to walk as far as
he could. After a couple of shaky steps, he fell down. Then he
crawled back to the couch, pulled himself up to a standing
position, turned around, and walked as far as he could until he
fell again. This time he managed three shaky steps. He repeated
the sequence several more times, and I was delighted.

  Look at that, I thought to myself. *He's determined to learn to
walk!* I stood a couple of yards away from the couch and waited
for him to make his return trip. I held out my hands to him.

"Good boy, Matthew! Mommy is so proud of you! Here, come to Mommy!" I gushed.

Matt looked me in the eye, paused for a second, and let himself plop to the floor.

He just sat there, staring at me, and I assumed that he was tired. I offered to pick him up, but he pushed me away.

"Fine. Have it your way," I grumped and walked into the kitchen.

I pretended to be busy at the stove, while watching him out of the corner of my eye. As soon as I was out of the room, Matt crawled back to the couch, pulled himself up to a standing position, turned around, and walked as far as he could until he fell again, each time adding a step or two. This went on for hours—past lunchtime, past naptime, and moving toward suppertime. Being a new mom, I started to panic and called the pediatrician's office. I just knew there had to be something very wrong with my child!

"Mrs. Fenelon," the pediatrician chuckled. "Do you want your son to walk?"

"Of course I do," I answered. "But . . ."

"Then leave him alone," the pediatrician said. "He's doing just fine. He's just a very determined little man."

That very determined *little* man grew into a very determined *big* man, and often I've looked back on the day Matt taught himself to walk, realizing that his crawl-pull-step-fall method was essential to his development, even though I found it hard to understand. At each new stage of his life, I knew that I patiently had to allow him the space to figure things out, even if it meant he took some bumps and bruises along the way. I did my best to nurture, guide, and encourage, but then I had to stand back and allow God to do the rest. It wasn't always easy, but I did have the consolation of reflecting on the way Mary patiently waited for God to reveal to Joseph the nature of her pregnancy.

A Difficult Journey

It's also worth considering what Mary did just after she told Joseph that she was pregnant. In spite of the grief and uncertainty she was experiencing, she traversed more than seventy miles of dangerous terrain in miserable and dangerous conditions in order to help her elderly cousin, Elizabeth, who also was pregnant. She did not allow her own serious situation to prohibit her from placing herself at the service of others. She knew Elizabeth needed her help, and so she went to help her.

On the flip side, I can see that Mary needed Elizabeth as much as Elizabeth needed her. With the confusion, controversy, and consternation Mary stirred up as the mother of a seemingly illegitimate child, there would be talk—and probably plenty of it—both behind her back and to her face. Her world had probably been turned upside down and inside out, and perhaps this was the ideal time to get away for a little while until things settled down a bit. Seeking the comfort and counsel of her older, wiser cousin could have been just the thing she needed. With Elizabeth's protection, she could feel secure and accepted. With Elizabeth's experience and advice, she could figure out what to do next.

Can you imagine what that trip must've been like for Mary? Can you imagine how much patience it required? On a physical level, it couldn't have been comfortable. Even though Mary wasn't that far along in her pregnancy, I could imagine she was experiencing at least some morning sickness. How was it for Mary to be bumping along on the back of a donkey with a queasy stomach? When I had morning sickness, I didn't even want anyone to sit on the couch next to me, because I couldn't stand the movement. Bump along on a donkey? I would never have made it! It still would've been tough, even if Mary was fortunate enough to make the journey in a cart or wagon of some kind. Some women need to eat every little while during their pregnancy, especially during the first trimester. How would that have worked for Mary? It's likely that she traveled in some kind of caravan. Did she bring something to nibble on, or did she have to ask the other travelers to make allowances for her?

In my mind, this must've been a lonely trip for Mary. I expect that she wasn't eager to share with the other travelers that she was an unwed mother. She had to bear that burden alone. If anyone found out, she might have ended up being stoned to death rather than returning home to Joseph. I often wonder if Mary had anyone to talk to beyond polite pleasantries as she rode along. Even if there was someone, how could that person really understand what was happening to her?

A Woman of Profound Patience

Then there's the question of what was going on in Mary's heart. It must have been horrible to know that her beloved had lost trust in her and that she couldn't prove her innocence. Joseph was back in Nazareth, and she was here on the road on her way to the home of her cousins Zechariah and Elizabeth. She had no way to communicate with him, no way to express her love for him, no way to tell what was going on in Joseph's mind and heart. Was he reconsidering divorcing her? Was he growing angry with her? Would he ever look lovingly into her eyes again? She wouldn't know until she returned to Nazareth. In the meantime, Mary had to focus on the task at hand—helping Elizabeth—while patiently waiting, confident in God's wisdom, and trusting that the truth would eventually come out.

For you and I, this would be a huge challenge, and it probably wasn't easy for Mary. Yet she managed to wait for Joseph to comprehend what she was trying to tell him about her pregnancy. She endured the uncomfortable and lonesome journey to Elizabeth's house. She coped with the uncertainty of her relationship with Joseph. She anticipated the unfolding of God's plan for her and for her marriage. She entrusted the future of her child to God's wisdom. All of these actions indicate that Mary was a woman of *profound patience.*

I don't know about you, but I can always find something to learn from a patient person. As a wife and mother, Mary is a natural model of patience. When it seems as though my whole world has been turned upside down, I think of Mary patiently waiting for God to turn her own world right-side up. Misunderstandings between my husband and I seem more surmountable when I take time to contemplate Mary's patience with Joseph in explaining her pregnancy. Praying to Mary helps me to remain patient when I anticipate what God has in mind for my own children, and to relax a little when I'm having difficulty clearly seeing God's will for them. Considering Mary's profound patience helps me to develop my own.

Enriching Our Motherhood
....

Thoughts to Ponder

Father, all-powerful and ever-living God, we do well always and everywhere to give you thanks.

By a wonderful and inexpressible mystery the Blessed Virgin conceived your only Son and bore in her pure womb the Lord of heaven.

She who knew not man becomes a mother; she who has given birth remains a virgin. What a joy is hers at your twofold gift: she is full of wonder at her virgin-motherhood and full of joy at giving birth to the Redeemer.

~Collection of Masses of the Blessed Virgin Mary,
Volume 1, Mary Mother of God

Deepening Our Motherhood
....

Reflection and Application

- Think of a time you had to tell your spouse some difficult news. What was it? How did you handle it?

- Has there been a time when you have had to let your child figure something out for himself? What was that like? What gave you the sense to stand back?

- In your own words, describe Mary's trip to visit Elizabeth. Imagine that you are a fellow traveler observing her. What do you notice about her?

- How well do you exercise patience? With your spouse? With your children? What manageable, daily resolution can you make that will help you be more patient with your family?

Becoming the Unwed Mother

....

Imitating Mary's Patience

1. Explain things carefully to others, and remember that they're not necessarily coming from the same perspective as you are.

2. Allow others the space to sort things out.

3. Seek counsel from someone who is older and wiser.

4. Surrender heartaches and misunderstandings to God.

5. Realize things aren't always what they seem.

6. Ask Mary to help you become a woman of profound patience.

Chapter 3

The
Handmaiden
Mother

Imitating Mary's Trust

In the sixth month the angel Gabriel was sent from God to a town of Galilee called Nazareth, to a virgin betrothed to a man named Joseph, of the house of David, and the virgin's name was Mary. And coming to her, he said, "Hail, favored one! The Lord is with you." But she was greatly troubled at what was said and pondered what sort of greeting this might be. Then the angel said to her, "Do not be afraid, Mary, for you have found favor with God.

"Behold, you will conceive in your womb and bear a son, and you shall name him Jesus.

"He will be great and will be called Son of the Most High, and the Lord God will give him the throne of David his father, and he will rule over the house of Jacob forever, and of his kingdom there will be no end."

But Mary said to the angel, "How can this be, since I have no relations with a man?"

And the angel said to her in reply, "The holy Spirit will come upon you, and the power of the Most High will overshadow you. Therefore the child to be born will be called holy, the Son of God.

And behold, Elizabeth, your relative, has also conceived a son in her old age, and this is the sixth month for her who was called barren; for nothing will be impossible for God."

Mary said, "Behold, I am the handmaid of the Lord. May it be done to me according to your word." Then the angel departed from her.

                                        Luke 1:26–38

If an angel ever appeared to me, I'm not sure who would be more surprised: me, or the angel! I think I would not only jump out of my seat, but under it I'd huddle, shivering, until some nice person came along to assure me I'd not gone mad.

I'm relieved Mary wasn't like me. As far as I can tell from the scripture passage above depicting the Annunciation, Mary may have been surprised—even a tinge fearful—but she wasn't chicken. She deliberately stayed in her place, open-mindedly listening to what her visitor had to say. I would describe her demeanor as calm-wonder. Luke wrote that Mary was "troubled" at what the angel had said, but she wasn't distressed. She was troubled, it seems, because she didn't understand Gabriel's greeting. The scene seems to me to be a peaceful one, and I'm impressed by Mary's trusting inquisitiveness. Obviously she wasn't doubting; rather, she was wondering. There's a difference. I can imagine that, revering and loving God as deeply as she did, and knowing that his love for all of his creatures is boundless, Mary may have been taken aback by hearing *she* was highly favored by God and blessed among all women. She may have been asking herself what she had done to deserve such honor.

We aren't Mary, nor are we the God-bearer, but we are God bearers in the sense that we carry him in our souls and have the mission to bring him to others—to help "give birth" to him in others' hearts, to allow them to see Christ in us and to experience him through our love. We are blessed and highly favored by God because we are "beautifully and wonderfully made" (see Ps 139), and for that reason God looks on us in a similar light as he does Mary. If women truly believed that, we'd have a completely different view of ourselves and of our vocation as mothers.

An Important Announcement

The angel then announced to Mary that she was to become the mother of Jesus, the Redeemer, the Son of God, the one who would reign over the house of Jacob forever, and whose kingdom would have no end. It's likely that Mary studied scripture—not as a scholar, but as a faithful Jew. She was aware of the prophecies about the coming Savior, but I could see that, in her humility, she never dreamed that the Redeemer would enter the world through her womb. Yet there she was, gazing into the eyes of an angel and hearing him speak those incredible words! Again, I can imagine her in awesome wonder, thinking to herself, *Why has God chosen me to be his Mother? How will this come to pass? What does this all mean?*

What if you were alone in the house, and God's messenger suddenly approached you as you were wiping down the kitchen counters? What if he told you that you would soon conceive a child destined to become the president of the United States? What's more, the angel tells you that this child would be *the* president who would turn our country around and lead it back into prosperity, morality, and godliness. Wouldn't you be shocked? I bet you would. Well, Mary's child was to become much more than an exceptional president; he was to be the Word made Flesh, God himself in human form. So, whatever you think you might have felt at the prospect of becoming a noted president's mother—wonder, awe, excitement, anticipation, unworthiness, whatever—Mary probably felt a hundredfold!

Mary's Response

We know from our discussion in chapter 1 that Mary gave her unreserved yes, her fiat, to the angel's announcement because it was her nature to say yes to whatever God asked of her. I think, for Mary, it was the proverbial "no-brainer." I can't imagine her having anything else in her mind but two simple words, "Of course!" Mary couldn't *not* follow God's will.

However, while Mary was perfectly eager to follow God's will, she didn't understand *how* it would come about. Being the Mother of God was an astounding privilege, but there was one not-so-small problem: she was a virgin, not only by her stage of betrothal, but, as some scholars believe, by having taken a vow of virginity. So, humanly speaking, becoming anybody's mother was impossible for Mary. But it wasn't impossible for God, and she knew that. That could explain her demeanor of calm-wonder. She was completely calm, trusting in God's omnipotence and wisdom, but wondering at how the seemingly impossible would become possible. This is especially remarkable when one considers Mary's youth—she probably was between the ages of twelve and sixteen!

If the conversation between Mary and Gabriel was to take place today, it might sound something like this:

"Hello, Mary. I have an important message for you from God."

"May I ask how you got in here? I'm pretty sure I'd locked all the doors."

"I'm God's angel; I'm able to go anywhere God needs me to, even behind locked doors."

"Um . . . Sure."

"Mary, God knows how pure and holy you are, and he wants you to become the Mother of his Son."

"Seriously? Whew. I'm not sure I'm worthy of that. But, God knows everything, so he knows that I'll do anything he wants me to. There's just one problem, though. I'm a virgin and have promised to stay that way. How could I get pregnant? I mean, doesn't that seem like a conflict of interest?"

"No problem. You'll become pregnant through the Holy Spirit's power. The child will be conceived and grow within

you, but you'll remain a virgin. God can do great miracles, and
this is certainly one of them."

"Wow. This is a lot to digest. But, if this is what God really
wants, then I'm not going to get in his way. I guess it doesn't
really matter if I understand completely how it will happen;
what matters most is that God knows, and I trust him. Yes, I'll
be happy to do this for him."

Again, I'm taking some liberty here in positioning the
Annunciation within a modern scene. My purpose is not to
lessen Mary's dignity, but rather to help you (and me) to get
to know Mary so well that we can almost hear her speak.
Knowing her well and developing a real, mutual relationship
with her is the key to imitating her trustfulness in our own
motherhood.

Mary's Choice

I think it's important to consider that Mary, like all human
beings, was given free will. She could choose for herself, and
she had the God-given right to say no to his request. She did
not absolutely *have* to become the Mother of God. Had she
declined his proposition, God would have allowed her the
freedom to do so and would have created another means of
our salvation. Pope Leo XIII said,

> The Eternal Son of God, about to take upon him our nature
> for the saving and ennobling of man, and about to consum-
> mate thus a mystical union between himself and all man-
> kind, did not accomplish his design without adding there
> the free consent of the elect Mother, who represented in

some sort all human kind, according to the illustrious and just opinion of St. Thomas, who says that the Annunciation was effected with the consent of the Virgin standing in the place of humanity.[1]

Not only did Mary say yes to becoming Christ's Mother for herself—in the sense of following God's will—but she also said yes for us in that her consent effected our salvation and is an example for us to follow in our own lives. Mary didn't worry about how God's plan would unfold in her life; she merely worried that it *would* unfold in her life and trusted God to see that it would.

I remember my first speaking engagement at a women's conference. When I received the invitation, I quivered a little. Well, more than a little. A women's conference? I'd never done a women's conference before; would I be able to handle it? I'd given lots of presentations, but none at an event of that magnitude. Would I be able to squeeze it in between my other projects and deadlines? Was I ready for this? Could I handle the responsibility? How would the audience respond to me? I worried, not only about how I would handle it, but also about how my family would handle it. Would they be able to hold things together while I was away? Was I asking too much of them? Worrying about all of that made me even more nervous.

I consulted with my spiritual director. His deduction was very clear: If it was truly God's will for me to accept the invitation to the women's conference, then everything would fall into place. According to him, the only challenge I faced was to discern whether or not God had worked the conference into his plan.

The next afternoon, I visited the Schoenstatt Marian Shrine near my home and spent some time in Eucharistic adoration there. I asked our Lord and his Mother to help me figure things out. "I'm just not sure," I kept telling them over and over again. I got about halfway through a Rosary and ended up falling asleep in the shrine. When I awoke, Jesus was still there in the monstrance on the altar, waiting patiently for me to continue my conversation with him. I felt embarrassed, as if I had let him down. I'd come for inspiration and direction and ended up slumbering instead. Then it occurred to me that, even though I hadn't held up my part, Jesus had continued to hold up his, and I understood that I should apply this also to the women's conference. Even if somehow I was unable to hold up my part, Jesus would hold up his; I just had to trust him to do so.

And he did. Although I still was quite a bit nervous, the conference went very well, and I actually enjoyed myself in the process. The women accepted my message with great enthusiasm and showered me with positive feedback after the presentation. I pondered this at some length during the flight home, and I realized that once I had committed to doing God's will, he took care of the rest. I never needed to worry.

I'm sure you've had at least one similar situation in your life. Were you offered an impressive job promotion and worried you might not be able to fulfill the requirements? Did you discover you would give birth to a child who would be mentally or physically challenged and wonder how in the world you'd manage? Perhaps you faced a major change in your life and didn't know how to accept it. These are all circumstances that might put you in the same state of mind that Mary was in at the Annunciation: wanting to do God's will in all things, but unsure about how that would happen. Let Mary give you your cue, and trust in God.

Parting Words

....

The closing line of the Annunciation passage is very telling: *Mary said, "Behold, I am the handmaid of the Lord. May it be done to me according to your word." Then the angel departed from her.* Mary called herself the Lord's handmaid. We don't normally use that word in the present day unless we're referring to medieval kingdoms or the Annunciation. A handmaid is a personal attendant, someone who is conscripted into subservience. There are two other places in the Bible that mention handmaids besides the Annunciation. The first is in the first chapter of Genesis:

> Abram's wife Sarai [later called Sarah] had borne him no children. Now she had an Egyptian maidservant named Hagar.
>
> Sarai said to Abram: "The LORD has kept me from bearing children. Have intercourse with my maid; perhaps I will have sons through her." Abram obeyed Sarai.
>
> Thus, after Abram had lived ten years in the land of Canaan, his wife Sarai took her maid, Hagar the Egyptian, and gave her to her husband Abram to be his wife. (Gn 16:1–3)

The second time is in the third chapter of Ruth:

> Boaz ate and drank to his heart's content, and went to lie down at the edge of the pile of grain. She crept up, uncovered a place at his feet, and lay down.
>
> Midway through the night, the man gave a start and groped about, only to find a woman lying at his feet.

"Who are you?" he asked. She replied, "I am your servant Ruth. Spread the wing of your cloak over your servant, for you are a redeemer." (Ru 3:7–9)

In both cases—Sarah and Ruth—we see the lowliness of a
handmaid. Sarah basically gave Hagar to Abram as a concu-
bine, and Ruth put herself at the feet of Boaz. Hagar had no will
of her own, and Ruth gave up hers. These passages demonstrate the gravity of the title "handmaid," and they shine light
on the fact that by declaring herself God's handmaid, Mary
conscripted herself into his service, offering to be his personal
attendant, so to speak. She wanted only what he wanted and
assured the angel that all God had to do was give the word
and she would do it, whatever that might be.

Your Handmaid

Mary wants to be God's handmaid, but in a sense, she also
wants to be *your* handmaid. Remember that, when she spoke
her fiat, she became the Mother of Christ but also your mother,
in the order of grace. She conceived you in her heart along with
Jesus. Saying yes to being his Mother meant saying yes to being
Mother of all Christianity, since we are all one in the Mystical
Body of Christ. Therefore, Mary wants to serve as your personal attendant in all your needs and concerns (according to
God's will). Her "may it be done to me" includes her ardent
love for her Son *and* for all those he loves—that means you.
Servant of God and founder of the Apostolic Movement of
Schoenstatt, Fr. Joseph Kentenich, said during a Lenten retreat
in 1954:

She loves us with a mother heart like no other heart that was or can ever be. Can we imagine at all how inexhaustibly great the measure of love is with which the mother of fair love loves each one of us so very personally? . . . No sacrifice is therefore too great for her love, no trouble too burdensome. There is no obstacle to which she surrenders. So that she can carry out her task, she is allowed to see us in God as if looking in a mirror—us and all our needs and cares down to the smallest detail. Thus one can say she is omnipresent through her knowledge of us and through her unlimited love for us.[2]

Mary says, "I am the handmaid of the Lord," but she also says, "I am the handmaid of my children." Mary wants to serve God by serving us.

Always Serving

As a mom, you can sometimes feel like serving is all you ever do. Perhaps you feel as though you're already a handmaid—to your husband and to your children. On days when you've been pulled and tugged in every direction, it can feel like you've been conscripted into subservience and as though you can't make anybody happy. At times like these, think of Mary and her trustful service to God. She said yes to motherhood because she knew it was God's will for her, and she wanted to participate in his plan of salvation for herself, for her family, and for the entire human race. By saying yes to motherhood, you said yes to God's will for you and agreed to participate in his plan of salvation for yourself and for your family. In fact, your yes also has impact on the entire human race, although not in the exact same way as Mary's did.

We rarely played games in my house when I was growing up. In my husband's childhood home, they played games all the time—card games, board games, word games; you name it, they played it. Once we had children, Mark expected that we would play games as a family because that's what was familiar to him. I, on the other hand, had absolutely no inclination toward game playing, and it felt foreign to me. Much to my misery, I discovered that the kids all inherited Mark's game-playing genes. What's a girl to do?

I learned how to play games! I wanted to serve my family, to personally attend to their needs and happiness. If they liked to play games, then I wanted to like to play games, too. I'm a terrible faker, so at first it was pretty obvious that I was gritting my teeth through every game. But gradually, the gritting subsided and I started to smile, and then laugh. I even initiated a game every once in a while. Eventually, I ended up really enjoying playing games, and now we play a game—even if it's just a short hand of cards—almost every night at supper time. If I hadn't made up my mind to trustingly become the handmaid of my family, then I would never have discovered the enjoyment and togetherness of family game times.

You can find ways to be a handmaid of your family, too. You have your limitations as far as what you can tolerate and accomplish (we all do), but you also have the ability to adopt Mary's attitude of subservience by the grace of God. It takes trust in God, prayer, persistence, and patience with others and yourself. When you pray, ask the heavenly Father to form you into a handmaid like Mary. Ask Mary to show you how she did it. Ask her to open her heart to you so that you can peek inside and see what it is that makes her such a willing, trustful handmaid. Then ask her to help you open your heart to her. After that, choose one aspect of your motherhood in which to develop your handmaidenness. I'd suggest not taking on too much at once; if you overwhelm yourself, you'll be more inclined to defeat. Find something to practice on a daily basis, and once you've succeeded in its practice, move on to another aspect. Little by little, you'll find great joy in serving for the sake of serving as Mary did.

A Woman of Profound Trust

Throughout her life, Mary was an example of perfect trust in God. She may have been somewhat baffled by the angel's request, but once she'd been assured that the request had indeed come from God, she put her hesitations aside and trusted completely in God's goodness and wisdom. Even if it didn't make sense to her human mind, she knew it made sense to God's divine mind, and that was enough for her.

Our own lives can be as—or even more—confusing at times. God may ask something of us that seems unthinkable, or undoable, and yet we may have no choice but to keep moving forward. The child who, in his early years, seemed so complacent and manageable suddenly became discontent and incorrigible, and you're left to wonder about the wisdom of God's plan for the child and for you. Your husband's job, once promising and secure, is now stagnant and unstable, and you're fretting about the future of your family. Your parish, once your family's haven of Catholicism, is undergoing changes that you see as intolerable, and you worry you may

have to find another congregation. Perhaps a natural disaster
has befallen your community, and the need is greater than
you could ever have imagined meeting. All of these dilemmas
require our trust in God's goodness and wisdom, for only he
knows what is best for us and what the future holds in store.

By meditating on Mary's unlimited trustfulness and allowing our hearts to take in all the calm-wondering details, we
too can become trustful handmaids of the Lord. As the Handmaiden Mother, Mary exemplified absolute trust in God at
every moment, and we see that so eloquently illustrated in
the Annunciation narrative. She didn't know the "how" or the
"why," but she did know the means by which it all would be
accomplished—God. Therefore, she may have wondered, but
she did not doubt. Rather than resisting that which she didn't
understand, she rolled up her sleeves, ready to trustingly serve
God in whatever way he asked of her. That's because she's a
woman of *profound trust*.

Enriching Our Motherhood

Thoughts to Ponder

Oh God, you chose that at the message of an angel your
Word should take flesh in the womb of the Blessed Virgin
Mary. Grant that we who believe t ayers.

We ask this through our Lord Jesus Christ, your Son,
who lives and reigns with you and the Holy Spirit, one
God, for ever and ever. Amen.

~Collection of Masses of the Blessed Virgin Mary,
Volume 1, The Blessed Virgin Mary and the
Annunciation of the Lord

Deepening Our Motherhood

....

Reflection and Application

- What is your favorite part of the Annunciation narrative? Describe it in your own words, and tell why it's your favorite.

- Can you think of other times in Mary's life in which she demonstrated her absolute trust in God? Describe them.

- What qualities of a handmaid do you already have? How can you further enhance them?

- What qualities of a handmaid would you like to have? How can you work toward obtaining them?

Becoming the Handmaiden Mother

....

Imitating Mary's Trust

1. Listen carefully when others speak to you; give yourself time to take in what's been said.

2. Foster an attitude of calm-wonder.

3. Remember that God will hold up his part even if you can't hold up yours.

4. Find ways to be the handmaid of your family.

5. Meditate on Mary's unlimited trustfulness.

6. Ask Mary to help you to become a woman of profound trust.

Chapter 4

The
Messenger
Mother

Imitating Mary's Obedience

During those days Mary set out and traveled to the hill country in haste to a town of Judah, where she entered the house of Zechariah and greeted Elizabeth.

When Elizabeth heard Mary's greeting, the infant leaped in her womb, and Elizabeth, filled with the holy Spirit, cried out in a loud voice and said, "Most blessed are you among women, and blessed is the fruit of your womb. And how does this happen to me, that the mother of my

Lord should come to me? For at the moment the sound of your greeting reached my ears, the infant in my womb leaped for joy. Blessed are you who believed that what was spoken to you by the Lord would be fulfilled."

And Mary said: "My soul proclaims the greatness of the Lord; my spirit rejoices in God my savior.

"For he has looked upon his handmaid's lowliness; behold, from now on will all ages call me blessed. The Mighty One has done great things for me, and holy is his name.

"His mercy is from age to age to those who fear him.

"He has shown might with his arm, dispersed the arrogant of mind and heart.

"He has thrown down the rulers from their thrones but lifted up the lowly.

"The hungry he has filled with good things; the rich he has sent away empty.

"He has helped Israel his servant, remembering his mercy, according to his promise to our fathers, to Abraham and to his descendants forever."

Mary remained with her about three months and then returned to her home.

Luke 1:39–56

Having been visited by God's messenger, Gabriel, it's now Mary's turn to be the messenger. She heard from the angel that her elderly cousin, Elizabeth, had miraculously conceived a child and was in her sixth month of pregnancy. Gabriel wasn't merely making idle chatter with her; there was a reason he told her about Elizabeth's pregnancy, and Mary knew that. God doesn't send a messenger in order to make small talk, and so Mary understood the angel's news as a call to action.

Only a Suggestion

Even though she was dealing with her own troubles—newly pregnant, and her relationship with Joseph in a crisis—Mary dropped everything and rushed to her cousin's side. The evangelist wrote that Mary went *in haste* to Judah, the city in which Elizabeth and Zechariah lived. This tells me two important things. First, Mary put others' needs before her own. Second, she didn't hesitate to obey even so much as a suggestion from God. Gabriel didn't specifically direct her to go to help Elizabeth; he merely informed her of the need. She got the drift all by herself, and she moved on it immediately.

I find it incredible that Mary didn't stop to consider the danger she was putting herself into by traveling without family or companions (at least as far as we know from scripture and other writings of the time). Most people picture Mary's visit to Elizabeth as a simple trek across town. Mary packed a few things in a basket, straightened up her room, and skipped on down the road and past the shops and houses until she arrived at Elizabeth's door, right? Not quite.

In fact, Mary's visit to Elizabeth involved a treacherous, seventy-mile excursion that took three to four days (about twenty miles per day). She may have walked, or she may have been able to ride on a donkey for at least part of the time, and she probably traveled in a caravan. The road on which Mary passed was no interstate highway with rest areas like we're used to when we travel to visit relatives. Rather, it was a steep road that wound through desolate, barren-rock wasteland pieced together by twisting canyons and cliffs. The terrain wasn't the only thing that made the trip so difficult and dangerous. Wild animals, including lions and bears, lurked in the hills along the valleys. In addition, bandits hid in isolated areas along the path, waiting to attack helpless travelers. The story of the Good Samaritan is an example of such bandit attacks, which often had political motives and were punished with the Roman penalty of crucifixion. Likely, Barabbas was this kind of bandit.[1] Can you imagine Mary and her fellow travelers running up against a guy like him? The thought makes me shudder!

Our Own Dangerous Journeys

You may not have made a dangerous journey as Mary did, but I'm sure there have been many times that you've demonstrated the same kind of devotion that she showed for her cousin. There are needs of all kinds all around us; you've probably encountered an array of them in people you know, either personally or through the media. Of course, the most pressing needs are found within your own family—your husband and children. When you're worn out and upset, those needs can seem as difficult to meet as the trip was for Mary to make from her home to Elizabeth's home. Sometimes a trip across the living room floor can feel as long and grueling as a first-century trip from Nazareth to Judah. Even when you're not worn out and upset, keeping up with the day-to-day necessities of family life can, in many ways, require the same stamina Mary needed when passing through the hill country of Palestine. When you have that kind of selfless dedication in your motherhood, you're being obedient to God's will for you, just as Mary was obedient to God's will for her.

Like Mary's travels to visit Elizabeth, there are some dangers in giving of yourself to others. You may not feel them, but they're there—they just don't involve wild animals and bandits (although I've accused my children of being the same). Nearly all moms have a tendency to overextend themselves, and that can pose a threat to our mental and physical well-being. By our nature, we're programmed to give of ourselves. We want to be of service to our families, to our friends, neighbors, parishes, communities, and just about every charity and cause that comes along, especially if it's one that involves suffering children—don't we? Unfortunately, sometimes we can give so much we end up completely depleted. Once we do that, we're no good to anyone. Mary gave of herself heroically by going to visit Elizabeth, and there was some inherent danger involved, but she didn't push herself so far that she caused harm to herself, and subsequently her child. That's a good rule of thumb for us, too. Giving of ourselves is good; giving of ourselves beyond our capacities is dangerous.

Beyond Capacity

Years back, I became the advisor for a women's house of discernment. How that happened is a long and complicated story, but the short of it is that I just couldn't say no. Originally, I had agreed to act as advisor, and I had assumed that meant an occasional visit or meeting. With my enthusiasm for young people, I felt that was right up my alley. Other people thought so, too. I had my family's support, and so I was eager to put my whole heart into it. Before I knew it, though, I had become the responsible party for the whole thing; that was much more than I had bargained for. Still, I believed in the project and desperately wanted it to succeed, so I kept on giving it my all. The trouble was, my all just wasn't enough. To begin, I didn't have much "all," since I had just burned myself out on another project (some people take longer to learn than others, don't they?). The stress began to affect my health, and I developed insomnia so severe that I would frequently go for four or five nights in a row unable to sleep. Believe it or not, even then I was determined to continue working on the house of discernment! And continue I did, until it caved in on me, and I was done. It was obvious to those to whom I answered in the diocesan offices that I had given of myself beyond my capacity, and by mutual agreement, I stepped down from the position. Not long after, the entire project folded, an unfortunate consequence of my inability to sense my own limits. I had failed to see the dangers of the journey.

Empty Time

I wonder what went on in Mary's mind and heart, besides considering the physical perils, as she rode along to Judah. I suppose there were many empty hours during which she examined all that had been happening to her. Was she thinking about Joseph? Was her heart breaking over the possibility of his divorcing her? Did she place it in God's hands and resolve not to dwell on it during her time with Elizabeth? Was she trying to figure out how she would support herself and her child?

Was she planning one more attempt to help Joseph understand what was going on? Or, maybe she was anticipating the way she would greet Elizabeth and how she would explain her pregnancy to her cousin. We can't know for certain what was stirring inside of Mary during the trip, but we can be sure of her confidence in God's ability to make the impossible possible and of her commitment to obeying his will regardless of the cost to herself.

Messenger of the Incarnation

How beautiful that the heavenly Father spared Mary from having to explain her pregnancy to Elizabeth! When she greeted Mary, the child in Elizabeth's womb leaped for joy, and by divine revelation, she immediately knew that Mary bore within her the Savior of the world. *And how does this happen to me, that the mother of my Lord should come to me?* With that, Mary became the messenger of the Incarnation. Additionally, Elizabeth recognized Mary as the most blessed among all women. Again, Mary heard that she was somehow specially favored by God. If the gigantic responsibility of being Christ's mother hadn't fully sunk in before, it was sinking in then. Mary's response shows us her acknowledgment of the greatness God had bestowed upon her and demonstrates her humble obedience in accepting it.

Mary's Magnificat

....

At that moment, Mary spoke her *Magnificat,* a prayer of praise, thanksgiving, petition, and supplication; a prophecy; and a history lesson all rolled into one. The first thing Mary did was to turn all the glory over to God; she took no credit for herself. In fact, she called herself his lowly handmaiden. Then she went on to predict that, because of God's greatness—not her own—all future generations would recognize her as the most blessed among women and that God would be merciful to every generation that fears him. Finally, Mary remembered how God led his people through centuries of hardship, including wars, famine, division, hard-heartedness, oppression, and unfaithfulness. She also highlights God's goodness, which was demonstrated by putting the proud in their place, dethroning despots and raising the trampled, feeding the hungry and depriving those with overabundance, and keeping his promise of posterity to Abraham.

There is some controversy as to whether or not Mary composed the Magnificat herself; it could have been an existing canticle that she spontaneously recited. Scholars think this because it's similar to the canticle attributed to Hannah in the first book of Samuel (see 1 Sm 2:1–10). Scholars also doubt that Mary would have been able to put together such poetic verse on the spot.[2] Regardless of who composed the Magnificat, Mary spoke it, and she meant what she said.

Rejoicing in All Things

The Magnificat offers us insight into Mary's character and also inspiration for our own motherhood. Its overall theme is joy. Mary rejoices in God and becomes the messenger of joy in him. She rejoices in bearing his Son. She rejoices in all that God has done for her and for Israel. She rejoices in being the Mother of all humanity. She rejoices in serving and obeying God's will. After Mary's example, we should rejoice in God and all that he has done for us and our families, in the gift of our motherhood, and in the privilege we have of serving and obeying God's will. We rejoice in the high points of our lives, but also in the low points, because without them we couldn't grow in our spirituality. As Mary herself proclaimed, we rejoice in everything and at every moment because it's all part of God's plan for our salvation.

Consistent rejoicing may not come naturally to you, but it is something we can all work on. One spring, the entire Fenelon clan simultaneously contracted a vicious stomach flu. With the youngest still in diapers and the oldest in elementary school, it was mayhem. Every one of us was bedridden, and we barely had strength to make it to and from the bathroom for ourselves, much less help anybody else. We couldn't make it to the store to get flu remedies, and so we had to call on relatives to shop for us and drop the supplies off at our back door. It felt like we were living in a leper colony. We took turns making our way down to the kitchen and back with supplies, sliding down and crawling back up one agonizing step at a time.

Once we got the stuff to the top of the stairs, it was every man for himself. We don't have a clothes chute and were unable to haul the laundry down to the basement laundry area, so the soiled linens kept piling up in the hallway. The pile topped my five-foot-two-inch frame! We were almost down to our last sets of sheets and towels when things finally started to settle down. While we weren't exactly *rejoicing* over our dilemma, I can say that Mark and I often looked at each other with a wan smile and agreed, "Well, if we all got sick together, we'll all get better together. That's a blessing, right?" At the end, we managed to offer a prayer of thanksgiving that at least we had one clean towel and set of sheets per person left. Now, of course, we chuckle over that horrible two weeks of influenza and praise God that we've never been asked to go through that again. Even in the most miserable situations, we can find ways to live the spirit of Mary's Magnificat.

Champion of the Lowly

I also find in the Magnificat a sign of Mary's strength and gumption and perhaps even a streak of rebelliousness. Mary was a member of the Anawim, or the poor ones of Israel. By uttering the Magnificat, Mary becomes their spokeswoman and, in a sense, defies the status quo. Some of her rejoicing is not only about what God has done for her and her people, but it is also about the justice he has wrought on those in power who unjustly exercise their authority. Clearly, she has a soft spot in her heart for the poor and doesn't mind seeing the rich go a little hungry. I picture Mary as the kind of person who would not hesitate to stick up for the downtrodden and to welcome those who live on the periphery of society. I can also see her charitably chastising anyone who mistreats the less fortunate or fails to help those in need. After having studied the Magnificat myself, I have Mary in mind as the obedient messenger of God's justice, the champion of the lowly.

Praying the Magnificat

Mary's Magnificat is an important image for me, especially when I feel that either my family or I have been treated unjustly. I will pray the Magnificat over and over again until the pain and anger subside, and then I remind myself of all the great things God has done in and through my family and myself, in spite of our lowliness. Perhaps this helps you, too, during those times when you feel as though someone's trampled all over you or your family. It's a valuable lesson to teach your children. Whenever things seem unfair or dismal, pray the Magnificat with them and remind them that God knows all, sees all, and is in control of all. He knows what's in every person's heart, and he will shame the haughty, diffuse the corrupt, and reward and uplift the righteous. We only must obey his will and allow him to work in his own time and in his own way.

Wanting to Become More and More like Mary

Luke's gospel says that Mary stayed with Elizabeth for about three months and then returned home. Can you imagine what it would be like to witness Mary's devotion to her cousin, her attention to every detail, her anticipation of every need, her gentle mannerisms and selflessness as she cared for Elizabeth? Can you imagine the excitement and joyful chatter as she helped Elizabeth to prepare the cradle, bedding, layette, and toys for John the Baptist? Or, the quiet, heart-to-heart talks by lantern light in the late evenings? Can you imagine Mary fluttering to and fro, making sure that everything was just right around the house? Perhaps she gave Elizabeth back rubs to ease the strain of the pregnancy on her spine or foot rubs to sooth her tired, aching feet. Did she sing songs of old as she arranged the cushions so that Elizabeth could get into a position comfortable enough to sleep? When I meditate on the Visitation, I can see all this in my mind's eye, and it makes me want to become more and more like Mary in her obedient service.

We can benefit from this image of Mary as we go about our duties as mothers. By imitating her tender caring and tireless service in obedience to God's will, we can be messengers of God's goodness to our spouses, our children, and to anyone else with whom we come in contact. It doesn't require a major overhaul of your life; it can be done in small steps, beginning by doing the ordinary things extraordinarily well with an attitude of joy. You don't have to do more things; simply put more into the things you already do.

The Visitation story shows us Mary as the Messenger Mother, as the first to bring Christ to others. From traveling seventy difficult miles to her cousin's house, bravely bearing the heavy burden of her tattered relationship with Joseph, and expressing her Magnificat, to putting herself at Elizabeth's disposal, Mary desired only to do God's will in all things and at all times—even when it came as a mere suggestion. From this we learn that Mary is a woman of *profound obedience*.

Enriching Our Motherhood

....

Thoughts to Ponder

"Joyful in hope": the atmosphere that pervades the evangelical episode of the Visitation is joy: the mystery of the Visitation is a *mystery of joy*. John the Baptist exults with joy in the womb of St. Elizabeth; the latter, rejoicing in the gift of motherhood, bursts out into blessings of the Lord; Mary pours forth the "Magnificat," a hymn overflowing with Messianic joy.

But what is the mysterious, hidden source of this joy? It is Jesus, whom Mary has already conceived thanks to the Holy Spirit, and who is already beginning to defeat what is the root of fear, anguish and sadness: sin, the most humiliating slavery for man.

~Homily of Blessed Pope John Paul II, Conclusion of
the Marian Month, May 31, 1979

Deepening Our Motherhood

....

Reflection and Application

- Make up your own Magnificat. What great things has God done for you? How has he shown his strength in your life? In what ways have you been blessed?

- Do you have the tendency to overextend yourself? What triggers it? How can you avoid or resist those triggers?

- What small steps can you take to foster an attitude of joy for yourself? Your family?

- What ordinary things can you work on doing extraordinarily well? How can you go about that? Choose one or two to begin working on right away.

Becoming the Messenger Mother

Imitating Mary's Obedience

1. Don't give beyond capacity.

2. Make good use of empty time; contemplate the ways God is at work in your life.

3. Rejoice in all things.

4. Pray the Magnificat often.

5. Be a messenger of God's goodness for others.

6. Do the ordinary things extraordinarily well.

7. Ask Mary to help you to become a woman of profound obedience.

Chapter 5

The
Young
Mother

Imitating Mary's Endurance

In those days a decree went out from Caesar Augustus that the whole world should be enrolled.

This was the first enrollment, when Quirinius was governor of Syria.

So all went to be enrolled, each to his own town.

And Joseph too went up from Galilee from the town of Nazareth to Judea, to the city of David that is called Bethlehem, because he was of the house and family of David, to be enrolled with Mary, his betrothed, who was with child.

While they were there, the time came for her to have her child, and she gave birth to her firstborn son. She wrapped him in swaddling clothes and laid him in a manger, because there was no room for them in the inn.

Now there were shepherds in that region living in the fields and keeping the night watch over their flock.

The angel of the Lord appeared to them and the glory of the Lord shone around them, and they were struck with great fear.

The angel said to them, "Do not be afraid; for behold, I proclaim to you good news of great joy that will be for all the people. For today in the city of David a savior has been born for you who is Messiah and Lord.

"And this will be a sign for you: you will find an infant wrapped in swaddling clothes and lying in a manger."

And suddenly there was a multitude of the heavenly host with the angel, praising God and saying:

"Glory to God in the highest and on earth peace to those on whom his favor rests."

When the angels went away from them to heaven, the shepherds said to one another, "Let us go, then, to Bethlehem to see this thing that has taken place, which the Lord has made known to us."

So they went with haste and found Mary and Joseph, and the infant lying in the manger.

When they saw this, they made known the message that had been told them about this child. All who heard it were amazed by what had been told them by the shepherds.

And Mary kept all these things, reflecting on them in her heart.

Luke 2:1–19

There is so much to discover in the Nativity narrative! Obviously, by then the angel had revealed to Joseph the true identity of Mary's baby (see Mt 1:20–21), and the two had reconciled their differences. Can you imagine how ecstatic Mary must have been to find out about Joseph's visit from the angel? I often like to picture Mary's return home after her visit with Elizabeth. I can just see her looking for Joseph, filled with hopeful anxiety, waiting for some indication of what he held in his heart. Had he changed his mind, or did he still want to divorce her? I've asked myself whether Mary went to see Joseph, or Joseph went to see Mary; I have a feeling that it was both, that somehow they met while on the way to see the other. I expect that, as soon as their eyes met, all of the heartache, confusion, and turmoil of the past many months faded away, and they were filled with a joyful knowing that everything had been divinely resolved. Oh, what a joyful, delightful embrace that must have been! And then there probably followed lots of nervous, endearing talk as they caught up on all that had happened in their time apart. How happy they must have been to be together again!

A Long Trip

Next they embarked on the trip to Bethlehem for the census. How many times, as they rode along on the way to Bethlehem, did Mary smile and offer prayers of praise and thanksgiving to God for revealing the truth to her husband? Because she was nearing the end of her pregnancy, this donkey ride must have been much harder physically on Mary than the ride to and from visiting Elizabeth. Yet it must've been so much easier to endure emotionally, so gratifying to be riding along beside her beloved, able to converse in love and honesty, to hold hands, to look forward to their future together with their new baby.

In Bethlehem, Mary went into labor with her firstborn Son. Think about that for a minute. Do you remember your first time giving birth? Do you remember the anticipation and uneasiness you felt? You probably read a lot of books and articles and talked to a lot of other women beforehand; and that may have helped some, but until you go through it yourself, you really can't know what to expect. In Mary's case, she'd never given birth before, but on top of that, she was giving birth to God, and *no* one had ever given birth to God before!

Checking Inns

As we've heard, they had trouble finding a place to stay because all of the inns were full with other travelers. A priest friend who has traveled many times to the Middle East once gave me new insight into this. The Palestinian people, he explained, are very hospitable and will generously open their homes to travelers because the landscape and climate can be so hostile and because it's their culture. Most likely, someone would've found a place somewhere for the holy couple, but the question was more one of privacy than of space. It wouldn't have been very agreeable to have Mary give birth surrounded by strangers—either for Mary or the strangers. I wasn't very keen on giving birth to my children in a delivery room filled with doctors and nurses. I felt so vulnerable! I can't imagine trying to give birth surrounded by strangers I might not be able to trust. How did Mary endure that?

Christmas Cards

Christmas cards romanticize the situation, but Mary and Joseph ended up in a stable, which probably was nothing more than a cave in the side of the hill. It was a dirty, smelly stable with a bunch of drooling, chomping animals. I'll tell you, Flossy's great for giving milk, but I sure wouldn't want her overseeing my labor and delivery. Yet that's what Mary had to endure for the sake of her child, and for the sake of God's plan of salvation. What's more, Mary's circumstances offered her no other choice but to wrap her sweet little newborn in swaddling clothes—basically, rags—and lay him in a feedbox. That's right—a manger is a feedbox. Can you imagine what that was like for Mary? Like all good mothers, she would have wanted to give her Son the best of everything. Instead, what she had to offer him was barely adequate. He was the King of Kings. He deserved a comfortable palace, but Mary had only the comfort of her own body and a bed of straw to give him. I can imagine that Mary didn't let this defeat her. She was being obedient to the heavenly Father's will, and she trusted in his goodness. She had been through other rough times, and she would get through this one, along with Joseph's help. She had endured before, and she would endure now.

Only the Best

The drive to give our children the best comes naturally through our nurturing instincts, and that's a good thing when it comes to their physical and spiritual well-being. Sadly, that instinct is relentlessly twisted and exacerbated by society and pressure from the mainstream media who want to make us think we're bad mothers if we don't give our kids the first, most expensive, most advanced, most attractive, and most popular of everything. This is especially so with digital technology, with which the pressure is on our kids to have cooler and cooler gizmos at younger and younger ages. Digital devices can be extremely useful, but they also can distract us from what's really important (holiness) and give us a false sense of inferiority. The best way to curb this attitude in your children is to first curb it in yourself. Do you put too much emphasis on material goods and comforts? If you do, your kids will, too.

You should want to give your kids the best, but the best that will get them to heaven and not the best that will raise their social rank. Mary certainly understood this, and so I can imagine that, while she may have wished she could give Jesus greater earthly comforts, she was content in accepting whatever the heavenly Father provided—for herself and for her child. Wrapping him in rags and putting him to sleep in a feedbox allowed him to share in the human condition, to get to know first-hand what his people had to endure. Perhaps giving your kids the experience of rags and a feedbox once in a while will make them more aware of the human condition and what other people have to endure.

During this time, there were shepherds out in the fields with their sheep. they, too, were in for a surprise. They were visited by, not just one angel, but an entire host of them! One of them broke the news that Christ the Lord had been born and issued instructions for finding him. "Let us go, then, to Bethlehem to see this thing that has taken place, which the Lord has made known to us," the shepherds said. So, off they went.

Fishbowls

Can you imagine sitting, quietly nursing your newborn, when suddenly a band of motley-looking outsiders arrive and ask to see your baby? An interesting experience, I would say!

When our daughter was born, she was a month premature and weighed eleven pounds and four ounces and was nearly twenty-four inches long. She was absolutely beautiful, but also absolutely . . . large. She needed some medical assistance after birth, and so she was transferred to the NICU. Because of her size, they couldn't fit her comfortably in an isolate, so they had to devise a special open-bed arrangement for her.

Needless to say, word got around the hospital that a little, five-foot-two woman had given birth to a baby of significant size. At that time, the NICU was positioned in the center of that floor, with windows to the hallway lining all four sides. Lo and behold, they positioned Monica's bed right in front of one of those windows rather than in a row on the interior of the unit.

And so, the circus began. Folks just couldn't resist wandering over to the NICU to have a look at "the huge preemie."

Because premature babies recover faster with lots of touch and affection, I spent as much time at Monica's bedside as I could—many hours a day—while gracious relatives cared for her older brother. While sitting next to her, I would gently stroke her arms and legs, and tickle her forehead in an effort to bring her some comfort among the tubes, needles, and restraints. I would talk or sing to her so that she would find comfort in my voice. Every little while someone would wander down the hallway, saunter up to the window, lean into the glass, and gaze wide-eyed at my daughter. Most of the time, they didn't even notice that I was there, until they caught my movement when I chuckled at the ridiculous expressions on their faces. Sometimes, I didn't like the looks on their faces and gestures they made, and so I would wave to get their attention, and then point my finger down the hallway in firm suggestion that they leave us alone.

On one especially rough day, I looked up at the window and saw a belt buckle pass by—a remarkably tall man was walking down the hallway, so tall that his waistline was at the height of the window! I raised my eyebrows, dropped my jaw, and stared. The belt buckle turned around and came back to our window. Then, the man leaned down (quite a distance for this guy), raised his eyebrows, dropped his jaw, and stared in at us. Our eyes met, and a look of embarrassment crossed his quickly reddening face. He straightened up, turned around, and scurried down the hallway, inasmuch as a man that tall can scurry. I later learned that the "giant" who had come to see "the huge preemie" was Milwaukee Bucks player Randy Breuer. His wife had given birth to their firstborn in the same hospital at about the same time as I had given birth to Monica. He had heard about us, and came to satisfy his curiosity.

Although Jesus was a curiosity for another reason, I can suppose Mary endured the "fishbowl effect" with her baby as I did with mine. How did she respond when strangers came to gaze at her child as she stroked his arms, legs, and forehead? Did they listen in as she tried to comfort him with her voice? Did she feel awkward at the attention? Did the "lioness" rise up within her, making her feel protective and guarded? Did she sometimes wish she could point her finger down the road and send them on their way? Or, did she want to chuckle at the ridiculous expressions on their faces? As a faithful daughter of Zion, Mary would have wanted to worship the newborn Savior along with the others. Perhaps she would've looked upon him in curious awe because of his God-Man nature. As the woman who bore him in her womb, she would have wanted to nurse and nurture him. Perhaps all she wanted to do was hold him tight, close to her, deepening the bond between them. Mary was the Mother of God, but she also was the mother of a human, cuddly, needy infant.

Pilgrims from Afar

We know for certain only about the visit of the shepherds and the Magi to see the Christ Child, but I could believe there were plenty of others. There would be family and friends, but also the faithful of Israel who longed for the Messiah and were open to the fulfillment of the prophecy. At times this was probably tiring for Mary, especially as a new mother who needed her rest. I bet she joyfully accepted these visitors because she knew

she held in her arms the yearning of their hearts—their Lord
and Savior. How could she deny them that gift? This, too, is
evidence of Mary's profound endurance.

Two or three times each year, the Fenelon clan's abode is
visited by pilgrims in groups of anywhere from five to thirty-
five. They're all members of the Schoenstatt movement and
come because, as a child, my husband, Mark, knew the movement's founder, Fr. Joseph Kentenich, and I had been consecrated to Mary by Fr. Kentenich when I was a baby. We've
enthroned the Blessed Mother in our home, and the picture
with which we've enthroned her was signed and given to my
mother by Fr. Kentenich. When the pilgrims come, there's
always a lot of hustle and bustle as we prepare. I have to admit
that it's a little stressful, but we're so happy to share our experiences of the movement's founder and the graces we've experienced through our enthronement of Mary in our home's prayer
corner, which we call a home shrine.

We know that the pilgrims come, not really to see us, but
to encounter the founder and Mary in our home shrine. So,
in spite of any inconvenience, we joyfully open our home in
welcome to these visitors. We're always extremely pleased
afterward, because we were able to give that gift to the pilgrims
and because we received so many blessings in return. I bet
that's how it was for Mary. In spite of any inconvenience, she
must have joyfully welcomed visitors because she knew they
were coming to encounter her Son. I'm sure that, afterward,
she was grateful for the gift she was able to give them and for
the many blessings she had received in return.

Out There

....

From time to time, we all feel as though God is asking us to be a little more "out there" than we'd like to be. Sometimes he asks us to step out of our comfort zone so that we can be instrumental in others encountering our Savior. It could be by welcoming someone into our homes, or maybe it's by becoming the visitor ourselves. Is there a friend you haven't seen in a long time? Do you have a homebound neighbor? Perhaps the Person you should visit is waiting for you to visit him at church. Your heart could be a stable for the Christ Child, and you could welcome others to encounter him there with your kind words, expressions of concern, promise of prayers, or sharing of your faith. Enduring a step out of our comfort zone can bring untold blessings upon ourselves and others.

As far as I'm concerned, the best line from the Nativity passage comes at the end: *And Mary kept all these things, reflecting on them in her heart.* What? Not the swaddling clothes and manger? Not the awestruck shepherds? Not the heavenly hosts singing away? Nope. All those lines touch my heart deeply, but the last line is the one that truly grabs it. That's probably because I'm one of those people who often speaks when she's better off keeping her lips buttoned. Awkward moments, unfamiliar situations, and long silences make me nervous, and rather than prudently letting them pass, I jump in and try to fill them, often to my own detriment. Based on the number of times Mary is quoted in the Bible, I think it's safe to surmise that she was not one of those people. Thanks be to God, too. Can you imagine what would have happened if Mary had been a loose-lipped chatterbox?

Oh, but Mary could have had good reason to be a chatterbox; think of everything she witnessed and experienced! I think Mary's disposition is poignantly summed up by the Holy Father:

> Memories of Jesus, imprinted on her mind and on her heart, marked every instant of Mary's existence. She lived with her eyes fixed on Christ and cherished his every word. St. Luke says: "Mary kept all these things, pondering them in her heart" and thus describes Mary's approach to the mystery of the Incarnation which was to extend throughout her life: keeping these things, pondering on them in her heart. Luke is the Evangelist who acquaints us with Mary's heart, with her faith, her hope, and her obedience and, especially, with her interiority and prayer, her free adherence to Christ.[1]

Great Composure

Mary experienced so much, and yet she kept herself composed, focused on Christ, and centered in the mystery of the Incarnation. What an example for us! Granted, there are men who don't know when to keep their mouths shut, but it's usually women who have a tougher time doing it. That's another way in which we see Mary enduring. Unlike many of us, Mary was able to endure the need to let things sink into her heart—to contemplate and savor them there—before she spoke.

In so many ways, Mary shows us how to endure: making the rough journey to Bethlehem in the final stage of her pregnancy, giving birth to Jesus in a cave, having only a minimum of comfort to offer him, being visited by curious strangers, needing to remain quiet so that the Mystery could remain in the foreground. In each of those situations, we can find examples to follow in our own lives, seeing Mary as a woman of *profound endurance*.

Enriching Our Motherhood

....

Thoughts to Ponder

Let, then, the life of Mary be as it were virginity itself, set forth in a likeness, from which, as from a mirror, the appearance of chastity and the form of virtue is reflected. From this you may take your pattern of life, showing, as an example, the clear rules of virtue: what you have to correct, to effect, and to hold fast. The first thing which kindles ardor in learning is the greatness of the teacher. What is greater than the Mother of God?

~St. Ambrose, *De Virginibus*

Deepening Our Motherhood

....

Reflection and Application

- When have you been unable to give your kids something you thought they needed? What was that like? How did you work through it?

- What is your attitude toward strangers? Why do you feel that way?

- In what ways can you be more welcoming to strangers?

- Do you fight the tendency to say too much, or too little? Why or why not? How can you practice having a better balance between the two tendencies?

- How are you at enduring? What simple steps can you take to increase your endurance?

Becoming the Young Mother

Imitating Mary's Endurance

1. Give your kids what they need for heaven, not what they want for popularity.

2. Exemplify a right attitude toward material goods and comforts.

3. Open your heart to strangers.

4. Be an instrument through whom others can encounter Christ.

5. Think (and pray) before you speak; take time to ponder things in your heart.

6. Ask Mary to help you become a woman of profound endurance.

Chapter 6

The Committed
Mother

Imitating Mary's Courage

When the days were completed for their purification according to the law of Moses, they took him up to Jerusalem to present him to the Lord, just as it is written in the law of the Lord, "Every male that opens the womb shall be consecrated to the Lord," and to offer the sacrifice of "a pair of turtledoves or two young pigeons," in accordance with the dictate in the law of the Lord.

Now there was a man in Jerusalem whose name was Simeon. This man was righteous and devout, awaiting the consolation of Israel, and the holy Spirit was upon him.

It had been revealed to him by the holy Spirit that he should not see death before he had seen the Messiah of the Lord.

He came in the Spirit into the temple; and when the parents brought in the child Jesus to perform the custom of the law in regard to him, he took him into his arms and blessed God, saying: "Now, Master, you may let your servant go in peace, according to your word, for my eyes have seen your salvation, which you prepared in sight of all the peoples, a light for revelation to the Gentiles, and glory for your people Israel."

The child's father and mother were amazed at what was said about him; and Simeon blessed them and said to Mary his mother, "Behold, this child is destined for the fall and rise of many in Israel, and to be a sign that will be contradicted (and you yourself a sword will pierce) so that the thoughts of many hearts may be revealed."

There was also a prophetess, Anna, the daughter of Phanuel, of the tribe of Asher. She was advanced in years, having lived seven years with her husband after her marriage, and then as a widow until she was eighty-four. She never left the temple, but worshiped night and day with fasting and prayer.

And coming up at that very time, she gave thanks to God and spoke about the child to all who were awaiting the redemption of Jerusalem.

When they had fulfilled all the prescriptions of the law of the Lord, they returned to Galilee, to their own town of Nazareth.

The child grew and became strong, filled with wisdom; and the favor of God was upon him.

Luke 2:22–40

It's hard to believe that Mary could need purification, yet she did—not because she was sinful and dirty, but because she and Joseph were a holy and devout couple, and they wanted to follow Jewish law. In the time of the Holy Family, the mother of a firstborn son remained unclean and confined to her house for forty days after childbirth, and then she would go to purify herself in the Temple. The firstborn son had to be redeemed, or bought back, because he rightfully belonged to God (see Ex 13:1–2 and Nm 18:15–16). So, in spite of the fact that Jesus *was* God, Mary and Joseph offered him in the ritual of presentation as prescribed. The ritual of purification of the mother meant purifying her uncleanness after childbirth, making her ritually clean again. Mary, a virgin before, during, and after the birth of Jesus, did not need to be cleansed. However, she underwent the purification ritual as an act of thanksgiving for God's choosing her to be the Mother of his Son. Usually, purification was performed in the local synagogue, but Mary and Joseph chose instead to have the ritual performed in the Temple.

The normal payment for purification was a one-year-old lamb, but an exception could be made for families that could not afford it, and they were allowed to make a simpler offering. In Mary and Joseph's case, the sacrificial offering was the lowest the law required: a pair of turtledoves or two young pigeons. This shows us how very poor the Holy Family was. They were unable to make the greater offering, and instead offered the lowest possible sacrifice. Likely, they lived in poverty, because Joseph's trade as village carpenter would not have earned much.

Attitude toward Authority

....

It's interesting that the Holy Family willingly followed the law even though they were perfectly exempt from it. This has served as a striking example for me, especially during times when I find myself struggling with authority. It's hard enough for me to accept rightful authority; when I'm faced with unjust authority, I throw a fit. My family teases me because, when I exercise in the mornings, the one song that really motivates me is the "Authority Song," by John Mellencamp. Suffice it to say that the most often-repeated phrase in the song is, "I fight authority." I think you get my drift. My mischievous clan has dubbed it "Mom's Theme Song," and I'm afraid I can't argue.

In the Presentation narrative, we see that the Holy Family courageously obeyed authority they didn't even have to obey! They totally submitted to God and gave to us an example of faithful service and commitment to him. Their faithful service and commitment continued for thirty more years, as they lived a simple, ordinary life together in their humble Nazareth home, continuing to follow the Jewish law and giving honor to God through the joys, sorrows, pleasures, prayer, work, and struggles of their everyday life.

Could you do that? Could you obey authority you didn't have to obey as the Holy Family did? What about authority you're required to obey, but resist? It's a valuable lesson to teach our children how to submit to rightful authority, and how to diplomatically oppose wrongful authority. It takes courage to do that, because it means standing up for justice and doing what's right.

Rightful Authority

....

Rightful authority includes natural law, civic law, and ecclesial law. Of course, we can't forget parental law! It's good to evaluate your own attitude toward these laws and then to examine what message you give your children by your behavior. If you didn't want to be a good Catholic mom, you wouldn't be reading this book. Yet some of us consider ourselves faithful Catholics and still have difficulty following ecclesial authority. We know we should go to Sunday Mass, but sometimes it's hard to give up that one, quiet morning when we might be able to sleep in, especially after a chaotic week. What would it hurt, right? It hurts a lot; it hurts our souls, and potentially the souls of our families, since it deprives us of the graces offered us at holy Mass. It's the same with the sacrament of Reconciliation. It can be hard to get there, especially if it's at an inconvenient time. But, we need those graces; we need the forgiveness of God and the absolution of our sins—and so do our families. The Church wants us to receive the sacraments frequently for *our* sakes, not hers.

The way you approach ecclesial authority will probably be the same way your children will approach it when they reach adulthood. If they see you joyfully and courageously rise on Sunday mornings; if they see you looking forward to attending Mass (squeezing in daily Mass would be an extra bonus!); if they sense in you a sincere need for the Eucharist; then the likelihood is that they will, too. If your children observe in you an attitude of penitence and desire for God's mercy; if they see you making a space in your calendar for Reconciliation; then likely they will, too. Following ecclesial authority is just one way in which you can show your children how to obey rightful authority as the Holy Family did. Developing an attitude of service and commitment in yourself will help your family members to develop an attitude of service and commitment. Courage isn't always about heroic feats; it's also about breaking through complacency to follow God's laws.

Wrongful Authority

The principle is the same for wrongful authority, although the approach is different. A primary example is the pro-life movement. There are laws in our country that allow for the desecration of women's bodies and the murder of innocent children. This, beyond doubt, is wrongful authority, and we have not only the right but also the obligation to courageously stand against it through charitable, diplomatic opposition. If you look the other way, your children will learn to look the other way. Not all of us are cut out to be sidewalk counselors, but we all can find some ways—even very small ways—to promote life. We can pray for those who are more apostolically active in the movement; we can participate in rallies, petitions, campaigns, or special events; we can fast and sacrifice for abortion and euthanasia victims; we can join in parish activities; and, most importantly, we can teach our children why contraception, abortion, and euthanasia are wrong. Again, we should teach our children the value of rightful authority, but we also must teach them the dangers of wrongful authority.

Symbolic Offering

Another critical dimension to the Presentation is that, when Mary offered Jesus, she was not only obeying the law in terms of the "buying back" of her Son and her own purification; she also was offering him in a symbolic way. Pope Paul VI explained this in his Apostolic Exhortation, "For the Right Ordering and Development of Devotion to the Blessed Virgin Mary" (*Marialis Cultus*):

> The Church has understood the prophetic reference to the Passion of Christ: the fact that Simeon's words, which linked in one prophecy the Son as 'the sign of contradiction' (Lk. 2:34) and the Mother, whose soul would be pierced by a sword (cf Lk. 2:35), came true on Calvary. A mystery of salvation, therefore, that in its various aspects orients the episode of the Presentation in the Temple to the salvific event of the cross. But the Church herself, in particular from the Middle Ages onwards, has detected in the heart of the Virgin taking her Son to Jerusalem to present him to the Lord (cf. Lk. 2:22) a desire to make an offering, a desire that exceeds the ordinary meaning of the rite.[1]

Mother of the Redeemer

At the Presentation, Mary is fulfilling the law, but she's also fulfilling her role as the Mother of the Redeemer. It's almost as if, as she presents our Lord in the Temple, she is saying, "Heavenly Father, I offer to you my Son, the child you asked me to bear, the child I love with all my heart, the child I will raise to the best of my ability beside my beloved Joseph, the child who is the Savior of the world. I wish that I could keep him all to myself forever, but I know that is not possible. He has come for the salvation of mankind. I do not know what the future holds in store, but I do know, Father, that whatever happens will be your holy will. Therefore, I offer my Son to you, for the completion of your plan of divine wisdom, regardless of what that means for my family, or for me. Take him, Father. I surrender him unconditionally to you."

Mary couldn't really know what was in store, and yet she was willing to courageously accept whatever it was. She knew only that Jesus had come to save the world, but how that would happen she had no idea. Her instincts told her to shelter and protect her Son, but her faith told her she had to let go and trust in God.

What a tremendous lesson for us as mothers! Every child belongs to God, every child has a special mission to fulfill as part of his divine plan, and every child will encounter difficulties and suffering. Our instincts compel us to shelter and protect our children, but our faith must compel us to let go and trust in God. It takes courage, but we can do it with Mary's help.

Mommy Vibes

It's been our custom to consecrate our babies to Mary after Baptism. In the witness of a priest, we offered our children to Mary and placed them under her shelter and protection, asking her to truly be their mother, mediator, and educator. As their father, Mark knew that Mary could provide for our children in ways he never could. As mother, I knew Mary could "mother" our children in ways I never could. Their minds, bodies, and souls were totally in her care, and they totally belonged to her. When our oldest son was deployed to the Middle East with the National Guard, our consecration custom was really put to the test. For sure, there was no way Mark could provide for Matthew, nor could I "mother" him. In fact, often we didn't even have contact with him. In my head, I trusted our Blessed Mother. In my heart . . . well, that was more of a challenge.

I would go through strange cycles of worry, when my "Mommy vibes" were resonating uncontrollably, and for whatever reason, I'd be thrown into panic about Matt's safety. Sometimes, it would be in the quiet moments when my mind wasn't occupied by the busyness of life. Sometimes, it would be in the midst of activity or a conversation. Sometimes, it was in the middle of the night. I'd suddenly jolt awake, head throbbing, heart pounding, and in a cold sweat. I'd be gripped by the inexplicable conviction that Matthew needed my prayers *now*. I would nudge Mark and tell him, "We have to pray for Matt, right now. I don't know why, but I just know we have to." We would either pray together or separately, silently. Often, I'd be unable to settle down again for sleep. So, I'd sit up in bed and pray a little prayer of consecration to Mary that I learned as a child, only I would substitute the pronouns with Matt's name. The prayer goes like this:

> My Queen, My Mother,
>
> I give Matt entirely to you. And to show Matt's devotion to you, I consecrate to you this day, Matt's eyes, Matt's ears, Matt's mouth, Matt's heart, his entire self without reserve.

As he is your own, my good Mother, guard him and defend
him as your property and possession. Amen.[2]

At times, my Mommy vibes would be so persistent that I'd
pray the consecration prayer over and over again until eventually I would be able to get back to sleep. It wasn't that Mary
failed me; it was rather my own inability to let go and allow
her to do the interceding, protecting, and sheltering that I had
asked her to do when Matt, as a baby, had been consecrated to
her. She could do it—I just wasn't letting her.

Ingrained

Do you have that same problem? Do you have difficulty letting go and letting God? When we are the ones responsible
for the care and education of our children on a human level,
it's difficult to remember that they don't really belong to us.
For nine months (or six or seven, if you took the shortcut like I
did with premature babies), we are keenly aware of the child's
dependence upon our bodies for their survival. We feel every
movement, every stretch, and perceive and know things about
the baby that no one else could. Until they can manage on their
own, we're the ones who feed them, bathe them, soothe them,
dress them, school them, discipline them, chauffeur them,
and lead them. Overseeing our children's well-being becomes
ingrained in us, and it's hard to think in any other way. Turning
them over to someone else's care might seem foreign to us. It
can be tough to remember that they belong to God, not to us.
As Mary and Joseph did, we should joyfully and courageously
present our children to the heavenly Father in spite of whatever
might be in their future. That's not always so easy to do!

Consecrate your Children to Mary

Perhaps it would help you to consecrate your children to Mary. It doesn't matter how old they are; you can do it at any time. You don't need a priest to witness, either, unless you want to. You can do it privately with just yourself and Mary. You could use the little consecration prayer above, or make up your own. You could even consecrate your husband to Mary, for that matter. How it is done is far less important than that it is done. By presenting our Lord to the heavenly Father, Mary set a prime example for us, and so we want to present our children to God through her hands in our own form of the Presentation.

Darkness and Pain

The appearance of Simeon and Anna on the scene turns this joyful event into one accompanied by darkness and pain. Simeon and Anna are devout Jews who become prophets when they encounter the Holy Family in the Temple. Simeon is filled with the Holy Spirit and understands immediately who the child is. He's so excited, that he takes Jesus into his arms and gives thanks to God for him. Simeon blesses the Holy Family and then lowers the boom. He prophecies that Jesus will be a sign of contradiction and that, through Jesus, what lies within men's hearts will be made known. Additionally, he tells the Blessed Mother that a sword will pierce her heart.

Can you imagine what Mary was thinking and feeling at that moment? This is supposed to be one of the happiest days in the Holy Family's life, and it instead became one of the darkest. There they were, with so much joyful anticipation, giving thanks to God for the gift of their child, thinking and talking about all their hopes and dreams for him, and then Simeon comes along and tips the whole thing upside down. I can't help but wonder if Mary was tempted to just pass it off as the words of a crazy man. But, she would've known better given that she was brave, faithful, and Spirit filled. How could she not recognize the work of the Holy Spirit in another person?

Dying by the Sword

We don't know what Mary's reaction really was, but we do know that she stuck around long enough for Anna to show up. She didn't try to escape the situation, she didn't try to interrupt Simeon, and she didn't try to refute what he was saying. Instead, she accepted it, took it into her heart, and allowed it to remain there for future pondering. What courage it must have taken to listen to the words Simeon was speaking! There are different scholarly and popular interpretations for the meaning of the "sword" referred to by Simeon. The most common is that it stood for the death of Jesus. Others suggest that it alluded to the discrimination Mary faced as an unwed mother or that the Holy Family will face because of Jesus, the fall of Jerusalem, or doubt Mary may have felt about God's providence at the crucifixion.[3] In my mind, it had to have been a combination of all of these speculations, although I have some difficulty believing that Mary could have doubted God in any way. Maybe her doubt was fleeting, lasting only a second, and the sword she felt was not the doubt itself but her regret at having had it. Regardless, Simeon prophesied that a sword would pierce Mary's heart, and we know that it most certainly did.

After Simeon, there was Anna, an elderly woman who spent all of her time in the Temple in fasting and prayer. Anna, too, recognizes Jesus as the Messiah and begins to spread this glorious news to others yearning for redemption. Again, Mary is confronted with the reality that her Son is no mere human baby, and she's reminded that she'll be required to make great sacrifices for the sake of his mission, according to God's will. Again, she handles it with poise and courage.

Through the Presentation narrative, Mary has left for us a legacy of courage. She showed us how to follow God's laws, offer everything to God, and accept bad news and dark predictions with backbone and determination. That's because Mary is a woman of *profound courage*.

Enriching Our Motherhood

Thoughts to Ponder

But the Blessed Virgin did not offer him as other mothers offered their sons. Others offered them to God; but they knew that this oblation was simply a legal ceremony, and that by redeeming them they made them their own, without fear of having again to offer them to death. Mary really offered her Son to death, and knew for certain that the sacrifice of the life of Jesus which she then made was one day to be actually consummated on the altar of the Cross; so that Mary, by offering the life of her Son, came, in consequence of the love she bore this Son, really to sacrifice her own entire self to God.

~St. Alphonsus Liguori[4]

Deepening Our Motherhood
....

Reflection and Application

• What is your attitude toward authority, rightful or wrongful? Why do you feel that way?

• Do you see your child/children as truly belonging to God?
  How can you be convinced of that, and how can you
  exercise that conviction once you've achieved it?

• Do you consider yourself a courageous mother? Why or
  why not? How can you gain more courage?

• What about the Presentation narrative most impresses
  you? Why?

Becoming the Committed Mother
....

Imitating Mary's Courage

1. Examine your attitude toward authority; foster and demonstrate the proper attitude for your family.

2. Remember that your children actually belong to God, and
   treat them as such.

3. Place your children under the protection, shelter, and
   education of Mary.

4. Ask Mary to help you become a genuinely courageous
   mother.

Chapter 7

The
Fleeing
Mother

Imitating Mary's Strength

When they had departed, behold, the angel of the Lord appeared to Joseph in a dream and said, "Rise, take the child and his mother, flee to Egypt, and stay there until I tell you. Herod is going to search for the child to destroy him."

Joseph rose and took the child and his mother by night and departed for Egypt. He stayed there until the death of Herod, that what the Lord had said through the prophet might be fulfilled, "Out of Egypt I called my son."

> When Herod realized that he had been deceived by
> the magi, he became furious. He ordered the massacre of
> all the boys in Bethlehem and its vicinity two years old
> and under, in accordance with the time he had ascertained
> from the magi.
>
> Matthew 2:13–16

Those angels! They're always bringing interesting news to
Joseph, aren't they? This time, however, the angel isn't bringing
resolution to a dilemma, but rather posing one. Herod wasn't
happy that the Magi had deceived him, and he wanted vengeance. He wasn't about to let anyone threaten his throne. If
this Jesus came to be a king, he might try to rob Herod of his
kingdom, and that just wouldn't do. Because of the Magi's
trick, Herod really had no idea who or where Jesus was or
how to find him. He did, however, have an idea of how old
the child might be. The most efficient way to deal with it was
to kill all of the boys in the region two years old or younger.
If they were all dead, then this king-to-be would be no more.
The angel's job was to alert Joseph to the threat on Jesus' life
and instruct him on how to find safety.

Role Reversal

What must that have been like for Joseph? What must it have
been like for Mary? Now, the roles are reversed from the
Annunciation narrative in that Joseph has heard something
from an angel that might be difficult for Mary to understand,
and he has the burden of telling her about it. This time around,

it's not about a new life but about the possible death of their child. How did Joseph break the news to Mary? In modern times, it might have sounded something like this:

"Mary, wake up!"

"Huh? What's wrong? Does his diaper need to be changed again? Could you do it, please? I'm so exhausted."

"No, Mary, it's not that. Jesus is just fine. For now."

"Wait, what are you talking about? What do you mean, 'for now'?"

"Mary, an angel appeared to me in a dream."

"Not again."

"He told me that Herod is trying to kill Jesus, and that we have to get up and head for Egypt immediately and stay there until he tells us it's okay to come back."

"I don't suppose this could wait till morning . . ."

"No, Mary, I'm sorry. We have to go right now."

Difficult Moves

I hate moving, even when I have plenty of time to pack and plan the move. I do like the idea of being in a new place, but it's the sorting through, deciding what to keep and what to throw away, realizing that we have way, way too much junk, disruption of routines, inconvenience of having things stored away, and that unsettled feeling in my gut that I get whenever we move. Transitions are hard enough when I've had advanced notice and know where I'm going; it must have been downright tumultuous for Mary! She basically had no advance notice, and, other than knowing which country, she had no idea where they were going. She'd have to rely on her inner strength to pull through.

Worse, there were no moving trucks in the first century! There weren't even any cardboard boxes! Granted, they didn't have as many possessions in those days as we do now, but there was still the sorting, deciding, packing, and unsettlement. There's some speculation as to whether the Magi visited the Holy Family in Bethlehem, or whether it was at a later date when they were back in Nazareth. Either way, sorting and packing were involved because they had to decide what to take with them, and what to leave behind. Also, they would have had to pack provisions—at least as much as they had available and could carry—for the journey. We don't know for sure where in Egypt the Holy Family went. The Egyptian city closest to Bethlehem is Alexandria—a distance of 312 air miles.[1] Folks in those days traveled at about twenty miles per day.[2] With twists and turns in roads and the trials of traveling with an infant, it would have taken them at least sixteen days to reach Alexandria. That's assuming they stayed there; they could have moved on to any number of other cities, all at considerable more distance.

Can you imagine packing up what you could fit in the back of your car and taking off to a foreign country where you (1) didn't know the culture, (2) didn't know the language, (3) had no definite place to live, (4) had no definite means of income, and (5) some government official had hired a hit man to kill your child on sight? Intimidating? You bet! Plus, in Jesus' case, it wasn't just one hit man; it was a legion of them! How strong Mary needed to be in order to follow the angel's directions without falling apart.

Resentments

As a consequence of her premature birth, our daughter, Monica, came home from the hospital on an apnea monitor. An apnea monitor is a portable machine used to monitor a baby's heartbeat and breathing. Lead wires from the machine attach to sticky patches with sensors that are placed on several spots on the baby's chest and abdomen. The monitor weighs about seven pounds and is roughly the size of a VHS player—not a monster of a machine, but it was cumbersome to carry around. And we did plenty of that. Because her heart or respiration could stop at any time, wherever Monica went, the monitor went. The only time she didn't have to wear it was when we were directly interacting with her.

Monica needed the monitor until she was about nine months old, when her brain, nervous system, and lungs had developed enough that she was out of danger. Before that was another story. She would frequently set off the alarm, either because her respiration or heartbeat had paused beyond the safety zone or because she had moved and the sensors didn't pick up her pulse or chest movement. Unfortunately, most of the alarms were real, and we would have to gently (and sometimes not-so-gently) stimulate her so she'd "remember" to breathe or make her heart beat again. Once, I had to begin infant CPR. I can't tell you how many times the alarm went off during the night, and we'd jump up, queasy in the pits of our stomachs, wondering whether it was a real or false alarm and whether there'd be a call to the paramedics that night.

As much as the monitor was a friend, it was also my foe. Even though it was there to save my daughter's life, I resented it. I got tired of lugging it around, tired of the wires and patches, tired of the odd looks in public, tired of the well-meant but hurtful remarks, tired of people—even relatives—avoiding us because of ignorance and irrational fears. Mostly, I was tired of Mark and me feeling abandoned and completely alone. No one seemed to understand what we were going through. I found it terribly hard to stay strong during that ordeal.

New Beginnings

I wonder if Mary might have felt like this, at least to some degree, on the flight to Egypt. The trip was necessary in order to save her Son's life, but it also was a hardship for the Holy Family. Until they found a place to stay, did they have to lug their belongings around wherever they went? Then there was all of the care of an infant on the road, which could not have been convenient. They were foreigners—I'll bet they received odd looks in public for the way they dressed and talked. Did they receive hurtful remarks because of their culture or status as they sought employment for Joseph and a home for their family? I can even see how people may have avoided them out of ignorance or irrational fears because they had an unusual background.

Things probably didn't improve once they settled in Egypt—at least not right away. New furnishings, new customs, new foods, new words, new ways of doing things, new . . . everything. Where did Mary even begin? Simple, everyday things like planning a meal and going to the market would have been challenging. Was she able to converse with the other women in the neighborhood, or was she lonely, with no other female companionship? Joseph was her closest friend, but women need other women to relate to; that's a crucial part of our nature. And what about worship? Were they able to find a temple in Egypt? Or, did their prayer and religious rituals all take place in their home, in solitude? Yet through all this, Mary exemplified strength, never wavering in her resolve to obey the angel's directions for the sake of her Son. When I think of Mary during the flight to Egypt, my resentment of Monica's heart monitor is immediately dwarfed.

Facing Adversity

Have you ever had to rise to an occasion that was wrought with difficulty and suffering? Perhaps you had to move because your husband (or you) got a job in another state or country. Do you have a child with a medical condition or an elderly parent in need of special care? It might even be that you were asked to take on something stressful and unfamiliar, like a volunteer position or parish ministry. All of these things are similar to Mary's flight to Egypt in that they require strength in facing the unknown.

What a fantastic opportunity to teach your children greater faith and strength in adversity! They'll watch everything you do and listen to everything you say, taking their cue from you in how they should deal with it. If you can muster enough strength and calmly accept what God is asking of you, you can help your children learn how to cope with the inevitable obstacles in life. Instead of resisting the change or burden, try to see it as necessary for growth—yours and your family's. Instead of rebelling, acknowledge that God is doing things in a way that

is different from what you would prefer; but just because it's
different, that doesn't mean it's impossible. Perhaps you can
bring yourself to approach the situation with curiosity, rather
than judgment. You might try asking yourself, "So, what is
my heavenly Father doing with this? What does it mean for
me and my family?" Remember that everything, absolutely
everything—even evil—works to the greater good in God's
hands. You may not understand why you're being called to
Egypt, so to speak, but you can trust that God will give you
the strength for the journey, and that he has something specific
and wonderful in mind for you once you get there. Helping
your children to understand this can make their lives so much
easier now and in the future.

Contradictions

Also in the flight to Egypt, we see how already Jesus is the
sign of contradiction as prophesied by Simeon in the Temple
at the Presentation. This is what the *Catechism of the Catholic
Church* says about it: "The *flight into Egypt* and the massacre of
the innocents make manifest the opposition of darkness to the
light: 'He came to his own home, and his own people received
him not.' Christ's whole life was lived under the sign of perse-
cution. His own share it with him. Jesus' departure from Egypt
recalls the exodus and presents him as the definitive liberator
of God's people."[3]

Was the flight to Egypt included in the sword Simeon said
would pierce Mary's heart? I could see that. I also could see
how the murder of the Holy Innocents could be included. Mary
loved God, and she loved his children (she still does), and I

believe that it must have grieved her deeply to discover that so many little boys had lost their lives because of her Son. Yes, it was part of God's plan, but a part that was most heart wrenching. How strong Mary had to be in order to accept that! The mere act of fleeing to Egypt was contradictory in itself— the one who wants nothing more than to offer all mankind a home in his heart ends up homeless himself. The massacre of the innocents was even more obviously the opposition of darkness and light. Jesus came to save humankind but ended up causing the deaths of humanity's most vulnerable. No one knows for certain how many innocents were killed by Herod's death squad. The Greek liturgy claims there were 14,000; the Syrians claim 64,000; and many medieval authors believe that it was 144,000.[4] Modern writers estimate the number to be much smaller—anywhere from six to fifteen or twenty. But when we're talking about such a cruel, senseless death, even one is too many.

Secondary Theme

Blessed Pope John Paul II spoke of a secondary theme to the flight to Egypt in his homily during Mass in the indoor stadium of Cairo during his Jubilee Pilgrimage to Mount Sinai on February 25, 2000. He suggested that the Holy Family had to flee to Egypt, not only to protect Jesus' life, but as a way for our Lord to symbolically participate in the exodus of the Israelites to Egypt in the time of Moses.

> In this way, Christ too, "who became man so that man could receive the divinity," wished to retrace the journey which was that of the divine call, the route which his

people had taken so that all the members of the people could become sons and daughters in the Son. Joseph "rose and took the child and his mother by night," and departed to Egypt, and remained there until the death of Herod. This was to fulfill what the Lord had spoken by the prophet, "Out of Egypt have I called my son." Providence led Jesus along the paths upon which in former times the Israelites had marched to go towards the Promised Land, under the sign of the Paschal Lamb, celebrating the Passover. Jesus, the Lamb of God, too was called out of Egypt by the Father to fulfill in Jerusalem the Passover of the new and irrevocable covenant, the definitive Passover, which gives salvation to the world.[5]

Jesus didn't only want to be *among* his people, to share in their nature and condition, but also he wanted to experience their history. Knowing that her Son had an essential, God-given mission, Mary—it's safe to say—boldly and freely participated in the sharing of his people's history.

God-Given Missions

All mothers are called to do that, aren't we? Each of our children has an essential, God-given mission, and our motherly duty is to freely participate in their missions by enabling them to carry it out. Sometimes that means accompanying them on their journey, and sometimes that means giving them a nudge forward. It takes courage, perhaps not in the way of facing danger or difficulty, but in being able to allow God to work in and through our children even when it feels like he's making a mistake.

During his senior year of high school, our middle son, Luke, decided that he wanted criminal justice to be his college major. I listened, asked a few questions, and encouraged him. Privately, I told my husband, Mark, "That's never going to work. Luke's a mass-communications major. His temperament is too sanguine and he has my media genes." Then, I stood back, prayed a lot, asked more questions, offered advice when appropriate, and let Luke move forward. Yes, I gritted my teeth, but I did keep my mouth shut. It was Luke's choice to make, not mine.

Luke completed the first two years of technical college and earned his associate's degree in criminal justice. Realizing that he would need a four-year degree to land a decent job in that field, he transferred to a university and began working toward his bachelor's degree in police science. I noticed that his enthusiasm for attending his classes had faded substantially, and he started second-guessing himself. For a while, he considered criminal law, then sports law. "He's getting closer, but he's not there yet," I told Mark. He found out about an internship with the local sports-radio station and thought it would be fun to try, just to see what it's like. He loved it. For the first time since he'd started college, I saw him eager to get up and get going in the mornings. He was on to something. Within a couple of weeks, he'd changed majors to—you guessed it—mass communications. "Bingo!" I gloated to Mark. Do I know my son?

It can be terribly hard to follow, rather than lead, our children along their life's mission. That's true when they're small and trying to exert their independence or learn a new skill, as well as when they're older and trying to figure out what to

do with their lives. I really fretted over Luke's original choice
of study because I feared that he would be miserable all his
life, stuck in a career that wasn't right for him. I knew he was
capable of success in police science, but I also knew it didn't
suit his abilities or temperament. Additionally, I knew that
the decision had to be his—it had to come from within Luke,
and not from me. With Mary's help we all can do this with
our children.

A Woman of Profound Strength

In pondering the flight to Egypt, we see how Mary stood strong
in the midst of adversity—puzzling messages from an angel,
hit men hunting down her Son, fleeing to a foreign land, a new
language, new foods, new culture, and a new way of life. How
much more could a mother take? Yet she did take all this, and
more, for God, for her family, and for us.

Mary didn't bristle when Joseph informed her of the need
for the Holy Family to flee to Egypt, as perhaps many of us
would have (yours truly included). Instead, she did what came
naturally to her pure and noble heart. Once she'd ascertained
that it really was God's will, she mustered her strength and
resolved to carry it out, and it was in following God's will that
she gained even more strength to carry on.

Mary knew that, as long as she was committed to whatever God had ordained for her and for her family, all would
be well. That didn't mean all would be easy, but it did mean
that all would transpire according to God's plan. Mary also
knew that God's plan is perfect, albeit hard to understand
and endure at times, and that God would provide sufficient

grace for everything he asked of her. Therefore, she could go on without bristling or fear. That's because Mary is a woman of *profound strength*.

Enriching Our Motherhood

....

Thoughts to Ponder

In dangers, in doubts, in difficulties, think of Mary, call upon Mary. Let not her name depart from your lips, never suffer it to leave your heart. And that you may obtain the assistance of her prayer, neglect not to walk in her footsteps. With her for guide, you shall never go astray; while invoking her, you shall never lose heart; so long as she is in your mind, you are safe from deception; while she holds your hand, you cannot fall; under her protection you have nothing to fear; if she walks before you, you shall not grow weary; if she shows you favor, you shall reach the goal.

~St. Bernard of Clairvaux, quoted in Doctor Mellifluss

Deepening Our Motherhood

....

Reflection and Application

- What is it about the flight to Egypt narrative that most impresses you? Why?

- How many times have you moved in your life? What were those times like for you? How did you react?

- What do you think it was like for the Holy Family to forge a new life in Egypt? Describe it in your own words, as detailed as possible.

- What are your thoughts about the sword that pierced Mary's heart? What do you think was implied by Simeon's prophecy? Why?

- What are some rough spots your children have faced in their lives? How did you help them to handle it?

Becoming the Fleeing Mother

Imitating Mary's Strength

1. Approach tumultuous situations with resolve.

2. Rise to the occasion by calmly accepting what God asks of you.

3. See adversity as opportunity for growth.

4. Ask God: "What are you doing, here? What does this mean for me, for my family?"

5. Participate in, but don't dominate or control, your children's life missions.

6. Enable your children to move forward on their own.

7. Ask Mary to show you how to have the inner strength that she did.

Chapter 8

The
Attentive
Mother

Imitating Mary's Hope

On the third day there was a wedding in Cana in Galilee, and the mother of Jesus was there. Jesus and his disciples were also invited to the wedding. When the wine ran short, the mother of Jesus said to him, "They have no wine."

[And] Jesus said to her, "Woman, how does your concern affect me? My hour has not yet come."

His mother said to the servants, "Do whatever he tells you."

Now there were six stone water jars there for Jewish ceremonial washings, each holding twenty to thirty gallons. Jesus told them, "Fill the jars with water." So they filled them to the brim. Then he told them, "Draw some out now and take it to the headwaiter." So they took it.

And when the headwaiter tasted the water that had become wine, without knowing where it came from (although the servers who had drawn the water knew), the headwaiter called the bridegroom and said to him, "Everyone serves good wine first, and then when people have drunk freely, an inferior one; but you have kept the good wine until now."

Jesus did this as the beginning of his signs in Cana in Galilee and so revealed his glory, and his disciples began to believe in him.

John 2:1–11

Oh, what an absolute joy it would have been to have Mary at my wedding! Not just because she could convince Jesus to make great wine, but because she'd have been right on top of our every need. Of course, I know that Mary actually was there—spiritually—but the thought of having her there in the flesh makes me wish I had been able to get married in first-century Cana. Next to the Visitation, I think the Wedding at Cana is my favorite Marian narrative because it brings Mary's humanity even more to the foreground.

Honored Guest

I can see Mary at the wedding at Cana. She must have been one of the most honored guests there because she was so kind, so joyful, so full of hope, so loving, so loved, and because she was Jesus' Mother. Wedding guests who didn't know her were probably drawn to her, simply because she radiated God's magnificence in every word, smile, gesture, nod, or blink of the eye. You know what that's like, don't you? Mary must have been like the woman at Sunday Mass who absolutely glows and is so obviously a woman of Christ that you just have to greet her in the vestibule afterward. You don't even know why or what you'll say; you simply can't help yourself.

Isn't that a trait we'd all like to have? We can, if we work at it. I have a friend who makes you feel as if you've just walked into the home of her heart. She is always happy, accepting, smiling, and upbeat. When you're around her, you just can't help smiling and feeling happy, upbeat, and accepted. She's the first one up to refill the cups when we're sitting around having coffee together, the first to extend a compliment, and the first to think of something positive to say about any situation—good or bad. My friend absolutely shines wherever she goes and obviously radiates God's magnificence.

You might be surprised to know that it doesn't come automatically for her. She has to work at it. Years ago, she made a resolution to bring happiness to everyone around her, and she prayerfully renews that resolution every day. In the rare instances in which she fails, she asks for the grace to try even harder in the future. She has kept her ideal in the forefront of everything she does over the years and has gotten to the point that her resolution to bring happiness to others has become an integral part of her identity.

Resolve to Resolve

You can do that, too, with small steps. Resolving to bring happiness to others might not fit your style or personality, but there are other ways that you can imitate Mary and radiate God's magnificence. Are you a good listener? Perhaps you can resolve to listen carefully to each person who speaks to you (your children will especially benefit from this). Eventually you may become the trusted friend in whose heart others feel safe. Are you creative? Maybe you could send handmade greeting cards or little gift baskets to people who are lonely, sick, or homebound. Eventually you may become the friend who reminds others how much God loves them. Are you talkative? Perhaps you can help others to learn the art of pleasant conversation. Eventually you may become the friend who brings out the best in others. You know what your "thing" is; consciously practice it one instance at a time. (Broad resolutions never work; they have to be concentrated and specific.) There are endless ways in which you can glow with God's love, joy, hope, and kindness. You just have to find one that's right for you and begin working at it.

Heartfelt Greetings

I suspect that, even though Mary's humility and simplicity might have caused her to inwardly cringe at the attention, she would have accepted it graciously. She probably saw each person as a child of God and welcomed him or her into her heart, offering a chaste embrace or a warm handshake. She would have recognized the soul within the body and reached out to it in utmost love. I can imagine that Mary probably had many conversations that went like this one:

"And how is your Aunt Rani? Has she recovered well from her illness?"

"Oh, Mary! It's so nice of you to ask. Yes, she has improved, but she's still struggling."

"I'm sorry to hear that. Would you let her know of my prayers for her and that I'll visit her next week? I'll bring some fresh vegetables and make something to help her feel better."

"Thank you, Mary. She'll be so happy to see you!"

"And now, how are you doing? Are you managing well? It must be a lot on your shoulders to help care for Rani and your own family at the same time."

And so the greetings would have continued, until everyone had shared at least a few words with Mary. I sense that, even in just a few words, Mary would have made each person feel as if no one else in the world existed. And for Mary at that moment, no one else did.

Dining with the Queen

Could you ever imagine yourself sitting down to supper with Mary? I think I'd be ecstatic, but at the same time so nervous I'd hardly be able to get down a mouthful of food! Still, I'll bet that, in her perceptivity, she'd be able to put me immediately at ease so that the nervousness would be gone as quickly as it had

come. Goodness! I wonder what it would have been like to be
one of the wedding guests seated across the table from Mary.
She would have found a way to compliment everyone and to
bring out the best in each individual guest. I picture her eating
and drinking with elegance and delicacy, insisting on being
the last to be served—at least among the group of people with
whom she sat. I even can picture this delightful Jewish mother
urging one or the other to take a more generous serving.

The Last Shall Be . . . Last

Oh, if we could find a way to foster in our children Mary's
desire to be the last one served! Meals, games, loading up the
minivan, morning routines, bedtime routines, and even chores
would all go differently. I doubt describing Mary's behavior at
the wedding at Cana would be enough to affect their conversion, but it sure wouldn't hurt. It might help to explain that
there would have been an abundance of extra-special foods
that folks didn't normally serve in their homes (like our weddings today) and that there probably was quite a number of
guests, so waiting to be served last might have taken awhile.
You can imagine things for yourself, and help your kids to
imagine it, too.

However, the most effective way to foster Mary's hopeful
and attentive attitude in your kids is to first foster it in yourself.
As a mom, it probably comes naturally for you to serve your
kids first or let them go before you in line. But what do they
observe you doing with others? Do you let other drivers go
first, or do you race ahead? Do you let the person with only
a couple of items get before you in the grocery checkout line,

or do you remain in your place? Do you stop to hold the door open for elderly people and other mothers with small children, or do you just go on your way? Dozens of these kinds of moments arise during the course of the busy week, and each one of them is an opportunity to foster Mary's attitude within ourselves and our children. Putting others before ourselves is a small, symbolic way of living our hope in the Resurrection—we show our conviction that something worth waiting for lies ahead.

Mother-Son Dance

Music and dancing were important parts of Jewish wedding celebrations, and no doubt that also would have been true for the wedding at Cana. The musicians may have played the lute, pipes, sistrum, and harp, or perhaps they played the lyre and zither. No matter which instruments they used, the music would have been lively and festive. So, I've asked myself, "Did Mary dance?" Dancing at the Cana wedding would have been different from the dancing at today's weddings. The dances would have been folk dances, gracefully choreographed and handed down from ancient traditions, and not suggestive and sensual as so many contemporary dances are. Therefore, I could see Mary joining in rejoicing over her Jewish heritage, the union of the wedding couple, and the prospect of the couple being blessed with many children—more souls to glorify God. I even can see her dancing with some of the disciples, and with Jesus. It's hard to imagine Jesus dancing, isn't it? But he cried at the death of his friend Lazarus. Why wouldn't he rejoice and dance at the wedding of the Canaanite couple?

Scripture doesn't mention Joseph's presence at the wedding, and so biblical scholars surmise that he'd already passed away by then.[1] It would have been a noble and beautiful thing for a son to dance with his widowed mother. What a touching, graceful (and grace-filled) dance that would have been!

Holy and Wholesome

This, too, is something that we can learn from Mary—how to appreciate entertainment in a holy and wholesome way. It's good and necessary for us to enjoy pastimes like music, dancing, parties, movies, theatrical performances, books, television shows, and games. God wants us to be joy filled and to value his creation. It's the kinds of recreation and how we enjoy them that matters.

Ever since our children were small, we've had family movie night nearly every Saturday night. We'd scurry through the after-supper cleanup, choose a movie (usually one from the library or video store but occasionally something on television), sprawl out in the living room with popcorn, pillows, and blankets, and watch together. The movies, of course, had to be suitable and interesting for all of the various ages in our family, and sometimes it was a challenge, but we always managed to find one that worked. That tradition has held strong all of these years, and even though our children are mostly grown, we still enjoy family movie night.

However, there have been times that Mark and I wanted to watch a movie on our own, one that we felt wasn't appropriate for the younger crowd. We would watch the family movie with the kids, say night prayer, send them to bed, and then bring out the movie that we wanted to see together. We thought we were so sneaky! One night, we realized we had been "discovered." As we were sending the kids up to bed, we overheard our youngest, John, then seven years old, complaining to his older brother Luke, then twelve years old.

"Yeah," he grumbled. "They just want to get rid of us so they can watch something only grown-ups can see."

Luke tried to console John. "Don't feel bad, John. I have to go upstairs too, see? It's just because they want to watch a movie that's not good for us to see. They're trying to protect us."

That hit me like a round of lead shot! What Luke said was actually the stark truth. The movies we chose to watch without the kids *were* meant for a more mature audience. They contained violence and innuendos that could be morally and emotionally harmful to children. So, we didn't let them see. But . . . if it wasn't good for our children to see those movies, then why was it good for us? The answer is: it wasn't. And it still isn't. Those movies, while not sinful, weren't holy and wholesome. It doesn't make sense to tell our children that they can't watch a movie because of its questionable content, but we can. Since that night, we've drastically altered our movie choices for ourselves and watch only those movies that would be appropriate for everyone—including the kids. We do still sometimes watch movies without the kids, but because we need the time together as a couple, not because they would be harmful to our children. Like letting ourselves be last, teaching our kids how to enjoy uplifting entertainment shows them that our hope in eternity is so strong that nothing sinful should ever get in the way.

Dressed to Impress

None of my research indicated that it was customary for first-century Jewish women to purchase or make new clothes for weddings—at least not anything like the twenty-first century, in which it's common to get a whole new outfit for the service and then another for the reception. Typical garb for a Jewish woman of Mary's time was a basic, muslin underdress with a keyhole neck and long sleeves. Over that was placed a dark-colored gown and then a veil. People (men and women) wore sandals of various designs. It wasn't customary for Jewish women to wear makeup, even for special occasions. My guess is that Mary wore her usual clothes, and her clean, fragrant hair was neatly tucked under her veil. Nothing special exteriorly—yet I believe she was the most lovely woman there. Her virtue, piety, and grace would have radiated out from within, making her irresistible in a pure and holy way.

Dressed to Embarrass

When I go to weddings these days, I'm usually in a state of unremitting embarrassment, not about anything dorky or clumsy I've done (although that is sometimes the case), but about the attire (or lack thereof) of my fellow women. It seems to be the prevalent and regrettable notion that weddings are occasions for dressing provocatively. When I look around and see women in these . . . um . . . outfits, I'm embarrassed—for them and for all of womankind. We are *so* much better than that! Women shouldn't be dressing like that ever, but wearing that kind of clothing to a wedding—a sacred, sacramental celebration—adds insult to injury. How ironic that apparel designed to incite lust is worn at an event designed to commemorate chastity.

It's bad enough to have women decked out like that at all, but to have them parading around in front of their children like that is a travesty. What message are they sending to their little boys? What example are they setting for their little girls? Just because it's a wedding does not excuse the fact that they are exemplifying immodesty and desecrating women's dignity. Is that really the way we want our next generation to grow up?

Whether it is wedding attire, or everyday clothes, what we choose to wear affects our children and ourselves. What we put over our bodies tells a lot about what we're like on the inside, and whether we respect ourselves and others. If we are filled with the light of Christ, and dress as though we are aware of that, then we'll illuminate the entire world with authentic beauty. That's what Mary did, and that's what we should do.

The joyous festivity, delicious food, spirited music, animated conversations, hearty laughter, and vivacious singing—I can see it all. What's more, I can see Mary at the heart of it all, surrounded by love, revelry, enthusiasm, and holiness. Yes, holiness. I'm convinced that Mary would have fully celebrated while at the same time remaining fully holy. What an example for all of us!

Mary's Request

It was at Mary's request that Jesus performed his first miracle, marking his entry into public ministry. I can picture Mary, who was ever attentive to the needs of others, noticing that the wedding couple ran out of wine—a major embarrassment for a Jewish wedding party!—and wanting to rescue them from shame.

Mary appealed to her Son, in expectation that he would help them. This shows Mary's hope in Jesus and in his divinity. Clearly, Mary is a believer in Jesus and has faith in his ability to perform miracles. What really touches me is the way that Mary convinced Jesus to give the couple a hand. She doesn't tell him that she wants him to come up with more wine. She doesn't try to con or dare him into doing it. She doesn't even ask him directly to make more wine. She merely states a fact, "They have no wine." And then she leaves the rest to him.

Jesus' Response

Jesus' response is surprising, at least to me. It was not the norm in Hebrew or Greek for a son to call his mother "woman."[2] It's possible that, by using this term, Jesus was de-emphasizing her physical motherhood and emphasizing her discipleship. Or, he may have been equating her with Eve, in the sense that a parallel can be drawn between Eve's request to Adam that brought the fall of man, and Mary's request to Jesus that signifies him as the Savior of man.[3] Either way, it would have been unusual for Mary to hear Jesus call her "woman," and I wonder if she found that hurtful. We can just think of how much pain we mothers suffer when one of our children addresses us in a sharp tone of voice. They may not mean it, but it still hurts. How much more Mary must have hurt, yet she didn't give up hope that Jesus would still perform the miracle.

Jesus goes further in his gentle rebuke of Mary by asking her, "How does your concern affect me?" According to biblical Hebrew, Jesus was basically trying to say, "That's your business, not mine." In other words, Jesus was not understanding, or at least was not acknowledging, that the performance of this miracle (and thereby of honoring Mary's request) would have anything to do with the work his Father had given him.[4] Furthermore, Jesus tells Mary, "My hour has not yet come." Here, Jesus could be referring to his final glory—his passion and Resurrection—knowing that performing a miracle in public would allow others to recognize him as the Messiah and therefore accelerate the approach of the crucifixion. He also could have been assuring Mary that, when his hour did come, she would play a vital role.[5]

Pain and Confusion

I can imagine that Mary, regardless of the meaning behind Jesus' words, felt pain and confusion over them. That wasn't the way Jesus normally spoke to her—what happened? Instead of reacting rashly, Mary likely pondered it in her heart, waiting for God to reveal the truth to her at just the right moment. In the meantime, she would not give up her hope—in her Son, and in the miracle she'd asked him to perform. Thus, she tells the waiters, "Do whatever he tells you."

While Catholics have for ages used this story as an example of Mary's power of intercession, most modern biblical scholars disagree. More likely, they say, it shows her unshakable hope in her Lord and her dedicated discipleship.[6] Like many other contemporary Catholic authors, I maintain that this was one more way for Mary to set an example for us and to leave us with words of profound motherly wisdom: "Do whatever he tells you." She wants us to do whatever Jesus tells us at all times, and in all things, just as she did. She wants us to have everlasting hope in our Lord, in his divinity, and in his ability to perform miracles in our lives and the lives of others.

We know the end of the story. Jesus did indeed turn water into wine. He saw six stone jars, meant for the rite of Jewish purification, standing there, and he told the waiters to fill them with water. Then, he proceeded to change the water, not just into wine, but into the finest wine the guests had ever tasted—120 gallons of it! Here is yet another symbol in the series. The water used for the rites of Jewish purification becomes wine. Jesus is like the water, pure and spotless, changed into the wine of the Eucharist. It's a splendid image, isn't it?

A Woman of Profound Hope

Throughout the entire wedding at Cana narrative we can see Mary's hopefulness. She brings hope to others in the way she loves, respects, and serves others. Her attentiveness to the needs of her fellow guests (as we could imagine), and to the wedding couple, is a sign of hope in and of itself. When Mary reached out to others, she shared God's love with them, helping them to feel their dignity as children of God, worthy of his love. Sharing God's love brings hope to others.

Mary lived hope in the way she presented and conducted herself. When done in a holy way such as Mary did, rejoicing in the good things of the earth—good company, good food, and good music, for example—uplifts hearts and minds to God. When we delight in God's gifts, we are filled with hope in his goodness and mercy. Mary did this at the Wedding at Cana as well as throughout the rest of her life.

Mary emanated hope in the way she related to her Son and encouraged others to relate to him. "Do whatever he tells you" is the tenet she's left for us—the one she lived by, and the one she hopes we'll live by, too, for our sakes and for our children's sakes. That's because Mary, the attentive mother, is a woman of *profound hope*.

Enriching Our Motherhood

Thoughts to Ponder

This Marian dimension of Christian life takes on special importance in relation to women and their status. In fact, femininity has a unique relationship with the Mother of the Redeemer, a subject which can be studied in greater depth elsewhere. Here I simply wish to note that the figure of Mary of Nazareth sheds light on womanhood as such by the very fact that God, in the sublime event of the Incarnation of his Son, entrusted himself to the ministry, the free and active ministry of a woman. It can thus be said that women, by looking to Mary, find in her the secret of living their femininity with dignity and of achieving their own true advancement. In the light of Mary, the Church sees in the face of women the reflection of a beauty which mirrors the loftiest sentiments of which the human heart is capable: the self-offering totality of love; the strength that is capable of bearing the greatest

sorrows; limitless fidelity and tireless devotion to work;
the ability to combine penetrating intuition with words
of support and encouragement.

~Blessed Pope John Paul II, *Redemptoris Mater*
March 25, 1987

Deepening Our Motherhood
....

Reflection and Application

- How is the way Mary dealt with Jesus' seeming rebukes
  a cue for us in dealing with our own children, especially
  when it appears as though they're heading down a way-
  ward path?

- What part of the Wedding at Cana narrative most
  impresses you? Why?

- How do you handle social events? How can you tune
  your actions and reactions to look more like those of
  Mary?

- How do you ask your husband to do things for you? How
  do you ask your children? Is your method effective? If not,
  how can you change it?

- What does it mean to you to have hope? How can you
  become a more hopeful person, a more hopeful mother?

Becoming the Attentive Mother

....

Imitating Mary's Hope

1. Choose and practice a resolution that will allow God's magnificence to radiate in you.

2. Examine the way you accept and give attention; work on making the necessary adjustments.

3. Foster a desire to be the last one served.

4. Enjoy wholesome, holy recreation and entertainment.

5. Be conscious of how the way you dress affects yourself and others, especially your kids.

6. Strive for hopefulness always.

7. Make "Do whatever he tells you" a tenet for your living and being.

8. Ask Mary to help you become a woman of profound hope.

Chapter 9

The Grieving *Mother-Child*

Imitating Mary's Faith

When the soldiers had crucified Jesus, they took his clothes and divided them into four shares, a share for each soldier. They also took his tunic, but the tunic was seamless, woven in one piece from the top down.

So they said to one another, "Let's not tear it, but cast lots for it to see whose it shall be," in order that the passage of scripture might be fulfilled [that says]: "They divided my garments among them, and for my vesture they cast lots."

This is what the soldiers did.

Standing by the cross of Jesus were his mother and his mother's sister, Mary the wife of Clopas, and Mary of Magdala.

When Jesus saw his mother and the disciple there whom he loved, he said to his mother, "Woman, behold, your son."

Then he said to the disciple, "Behold, your mother." And from that hour the disciple took her into his home.

After this, aware that everything was now finished, in order that the scripture might be fulfilled, Jesus said, "I thirst."

There was a vessel filled with common wine. So they put a sponge soaked in wine on a sprig of hyssop and put it up to his mouth.

When Jesus had taken the wine, he said, "It is finished." And bowing his head, he handed over the spirit.

John 19:23–30

I think it's very common to contemplate the image of Mary at the foot of the Cross without considering the events that immediately preceded it. Jesus' trial, scourging, condemnation, and carrying of the Cross on the road to Calvary were all a part of Mary's experience as a grieving mother. She accompanied her Son during each vicious blow, vulgar insult, flail of the whip, stumbling step, tumbling fall, and drop of blood. Each of these torments was probably heart-wrenching for Mary to endure. Just imagine as a mother yourself what it would be like to watch your child endure the most painful torture known to man. It would be unbearable.

Watch Wait Pray.

Mary had to watch . . . and wait . . . and pray, as her Son was falsely accused, given a bogus trial, and then put before a hostile mob for sentencing. What a helpless feeling that must have been! It wasn't as if Mary could hire a lawyer to plead Jesus' case, do a little plea bargaining, and negotiate a lighter sentence. There was no defense for Jesus, save that which he could—but would not—offer himself. Did Mary question why her Son wouldn't speak in his own defense? She knew he was perfectly capable. Not only that, but he could change the entire course of events with the blink of an eye. Can you imagine the suspense, the fretting, the tension that Mary experienced during this time? I can see her standing someplace in the crowd, being jostled back and forth by her Son's foes. Perhaps some of them recognized her as Jesus' mother, and cursed and spat on her. Maybe she was even struck a couple of times. Was she muttering, "Jesus, *do* something!" under her breath? No doubt, at a deeper level, she knew the answer. She knew that Jesus wouldn't do anything, because there wasn't anything left to do but follow the heavenly Father's will.

False Accusations

It's a horrible, sinking feeling to have a child falsely accused. When Monica was a new nursing student, she got a job at a local nursing home. It was exciting for her to be working in her field, even if it was simply as a certified nursing assistant. She was good at her job, and she loved it—at least initially (CNA). Then, she started to notice things that were troubling, like neglect, mistreatment, and even abuse of patients. She saw other employees—even some of the nurses—doing things against regulations, and so she spoke up about it hoping to make a positive change.

One day, an elderly woman who was under Monica's care was injured. It wasn't life threatening, but it did require medical attention. The injury actually occurred while the woman was under the supervision of another CNA in the recreation room, and it happened because one of the nurses had failed to provide the woman with the necessary protective equipment, even though Monica had asked several times. Regardless, Monica was held responsible for the woman's injury, even to the point that the case went to the state, which accused her of intentionally injuring the resident—impossible, since Monica wasn't even in the room when the woman was injured! Someone knew how that elderly woman had been injured, but *no one* would tell the truth. Instead, they let Monica take the fall. Thanks be to God, she has moved on from that, recovered her good standing, and is now a dean's list nursing student working her way through clinicals.

I daresay that Monica handled the situation far better than I did. I was ready to beg, borrow, and—well, not really steal, but you get the idea—to come up with the tens of thousands of dollars it would've cost to fight the case in court. Monica instead chose a different route, which was a much more mature and fruitful decision than I would have made. Me? I was infuriated at the thought that anyone would falsely accuse my child of anything, especially of such a serious offense that could possibly ruin her future career. I was blinded by my own anger and pride.

Monica's experiences with the false accusations from the nursing home give me some insight into what Mary must have felt at Jesus' trial with Pilate. I can imagine that Mary may have felt anger, but I can't imagine that she would have been blinded by it. Certainly, she would not have been overcome with pride as I was. She would have remained faithful to God's will in all things, even this.

At the Scourging

Was Mary at Jesus' scourging? It's not apparent in scripture, yet there are saints who claim that she was. Among them is Blessed Anne Catherine Emmerich (1774–1824), an Augustian nun, mystic, visionary, and stigmatist who lived in Wesphalia, Germany. She dictated a series of meditations on our Lord's passion that were recorded and compiled into a collection titled *The Dolorous Passion of Our Lord Jesus Christ*. She described Mary's presence at the scourging in this way:

> Jesus trembled and shuddered as he stood before the pillar, and took off his garments as quickly as he could, but his hands were bloody and swollen. The only return he made when his brutal executioners struck and abused him was to pray for them in the most touching manner: he turned his face once towards his Mother, who was standing overcome with grief; this look quite unnerved her: she fainted, and would have fallen, had not the holy women who were there supported her.[1]

I have no trouble believing that Mary would have done everything in her power to be present at the scourging and that her response would have resembled the depiction given by Blessed Anne Catherine Emmerich. What would you have done? Would you have been able to stand strong, faithfully accepting it all without caving in? I don't think I would have. But Mary did. She stood strong—or at least as strong as her human nature would allow her to—and accepted the scourging in faith, confident that all was unfolding according to God's plan, no matter how absurd it might all seem.

Before the Mob

Jesus was led away after the scourging; when Mary next saw him, he was again with Pilate before the mob, this time wearing a crown of thorns that had perforated his skull. There was her Son, held up for public ridicule, his flesh torn, raw, and bleeding. Once again Pilate insisted that he didn't find Jesus guilty of any crime. Once again the mob demanded his crucifixion. Once again Mary felt faint. Can we ever really imagine what that was like?

One day, I was working around the house when Matthew, then eight years old, burst in the front door, took a few steps, and fell onto the seat on the front porch. He was making a chilling moaning sound, and his speech was unrecognizable. His eyes were glassy and rolling to the back of his head. All I could get out of him was something about his bike. He started writhing in pain, and then I saw it—a huge, skinned area on the back of his head. I told him not to move, ran to the kitchen, soaked a towel in cold water, ran back to Matt, and wrapped his head in the towel, hoping that would give him some relief. Then I called Mark home from work. Thank goodness, he worked close to home, and we were able to get Matt into the urgent-care center in no time. Matt had indeed taken a spill on his bike and suffered a severe concussion as a result. His recovery took a while, but he did recover in full.

When Matt came into the house, my head and heart began to pound wildly; I knew something was very wrong because he had never made sounds or acted like that before. When I turned him over and saw all that raw, bleeding skin on the back of his head, I felt faint. I think the only thing that kept me from losing it was the awareness that I was the only one around, and Matt was depending entirely on me. So I can understand, in my own small way, how Mary could have felt faint at Jesus' scourging and crowning with thorns and yet knew that he needed her to be there.

Only the Beginning

Tragically, the ordeal had only begun. Jesus now had to carry the heavy beam of the Cross all the way up the hill to Calvary. In his condition, carrying a broomstick would have been unmanageable. The idea of a maliciously wounded man carrying a solid, wooden cross large enough to hold an average-sized man up a steep, rocky hill is mind boggling. Now, imagine that man's mother following him, unable to help him in any way; that's even more mind boggling.

You know how hard it is to see your child struggling to accomplish a difficult task, like learning a new concept, for example. You might demonstrate or explain it, practice it with your child, and then give your child a chance to try it on his own. All the while, you continue to encourage your child in developing this new ability. Yet in spite of your best efforts, the child just doesn't catch on. He gets frustrated and wants to quit, but you convince him not to give up, to try again—and again and again, if necessary. You know that you can only lead him so far, and that in the end he has to figure it out for himself. Observing the process can push you right to your limit—perhaps even beyond. When you consider how distressing it can be to observe your child grappling with something that's hard for him, you can imagine how much more distressing it was for Mary to observe Jesus trying to make it up that hill with his Cross.

The Paradox

What a predicament for Mary! The way of the Cross was agonizing, but the crucifixion awaiting Jesus on Golgotha would be indescribably excruciating. Prolonging the climb up the hill would multiply the anguish of the ascent; rushing it would accelerate the approach of the most torturous of deaths. It may seem trite, but in this moment I can only think of one phrase, *the* phrase I use whenever I'm faced with tribulation and suffering: There's no way out but through. Only by proceeding could the unspeakable torment finally end.

In my Marian Stations of the Cross, *Ecce Mater Tua–Behold, Your Mother*, I describe the moment of crucifixion in this way:

> The strokes of the executioner's hammer pound right through my heart. Jesus must have swung his carpenter's

hammer countless times over the wood, forcing the nails to penetrate and thus create something beautiful. As he worked, did he ever think of the nails that would some-day penetrate his own flesh and bind it against the wood? Blood spurts forth from the hands that have so often built, blessed, and healed. The executioner is Satan's instrument of destruction. He doesn't know he's really creating some-thing indescribably beautiful—our salvation.[2]

We can't really know what was going on in Mary's mind as she watched Jesus being so brutally murdered. But, as mothers, I think we can get some idea of what was going on in her heart.

That's Enough!

When my youngest son, John, was a year old, I took him for a wellness checkup at the clinic. At that time, there was a state law that required doctors to annually test for lead levels in children beginning at twelve months. The test required a blood draw, which, of course, meant a needle inserted into the vein in the crook of the arm. I was hesitant, but since it was a law, I consented. The nurse who was assigned to draw John's blood was very new to her job and obviously very nervous. I tried to be as reassuring as I could, and I did my best to distract John and keep him still as the nurse worked on him. At the first poke, John jumped a little and started to cry, so I held him more tightly. Then, he started to wiggle around, and I had to restrain him. He started to scream. The nurse couldn't find the vein, and so she proceeded to pull the needle in and out, shifting it back and forth under John's skin. After a third try,

I was literally in a sweat and strongly suggested to the nurse that we wait and try again another day.

"No! I can do it!" She insisted as she continued pulling and shifting the needle in John's arm. John went wild with pain as his arm began to swell and bruise.

"No," I demanded. "This isn't going to work—can't you see?"

"Let me try one more time!" She persisted.

I could take it no longer. John was nearly purple from crying and screaming. I was nearly purple with rage. I leaned toward the nurse's face, looked her directly in the eyes, and shouted, "That is enough! Take that needle out of my son *now!*"

Believe it or not, I could tell she was tempted to try just one last time, but by now she knew I meant what I said. With an agitated sigh, she pulled the needle out and laid it on the tray. Two other nurses had entered the room because they heard the commotion. I scooped John up in my arms and glared at all three of them.

As calmly as I could, I said, "Ladies, we are all done here today. Not ever again shall my son come through the doors of this clinic." I brushed past them—maybe a little more than a brush—and walked out the door, never to return.

I can imagine Mary feeling much the same way at the crucifixion. Did she want to scream, "That is enough!"? Did she want to gather up her Son, walk boldly past his executioners, and take him home? Oh, I have no doubt that she did! But she couldn't. She could only wait there in faith, suffering it all along with him, praying for God's strength for herself and Jesus, and for God's mercy for the bloodthirsty soldiers. The difference between Mary and me, however, is that Mary in her holiness, not only understood, but truly believed that what was unraveling before her eyes was good and necessary, in the sense that it was essential for the salvation of mankind. I believe, but my faith is nowhere near as strong as Mary's.

You must know that feeling, too. Most mothers do, at one time or another. Was there a time when something unpleasant was happening to your child, and you wanted to scream, "That's enough!"? Did you want to scoop him up and carry him home? Perhaps it was a painful medical procedure, or some kind of an emotional crisis. Maybe your child is going through something unpleasant right now, and you want to stop it, but you can't. Take consolation in knowing that Mary understands exactly how you feel, because she's been there herself. Let her lead you through it in faith.

Jesus' Tunic

There's speculation that Mary made the tunic for which the soldiers cast lots at the crucifixion. That can't be definitively proven, but I can certainly imagine it is true, can't you? Our Lord didn't have a wife, or even any sisters, to make his clothing, so why wouldn't Mary be happy to do that for him? Of course she would! If Mary had made the tunic, it would have been with the utmost care and skill, entwined with her love and devotion for her Son. Maybe it was the last thing she had ever made for him. Would she have made certain that it would fit exactly right, with fabric that was durable yet soft? Would she have prayed over it as she worked, invoking God's blessing and protection for its wearer? Would she have pictured the places and occasions at which he would wear it? I can see all of that, and more.

Even if Mary had not made Jesus' tunic, I expect that it would have vastly disturbed her to see it ripped from Jesus' bruised, bleeding, and tortured body, gambled over, and snatched by some callous, heathen soldier. The tunic—regardless who made it—would have been meaningful to her because it belonged to her Son. It was something that he wore on his body, that his sacred hands had touched countless times, that had been part of his daily routine. To have any of Jesus' possessions treated in such manner would have cut deeply into that holy Mother's heart, don't you think? Perhaps it evoked anger, even rage at the injustice and disrespect for her Son, her Lord. However, I also can see that Mary, in spite of her wounded heart, would have accepted this in faith. Nothing, not even evil, happens without reason. God oversees all, down to the smallest detail, including the casting of lots for a tunic.

Recalling the Psalms

We can tell from her Magnificat that Mary knew scripture, so we can assume that she was familiar with the Psalms. Perhaps, as she watched the soldiers vying for Jesus' tunic, Psalm 22 came to her mind:

> Dogs surround me; a pack of evildoers closes in on me. They have pierced my hands and my feet. I can count all my bones. They stare at me and gloat; they divide my garments among them; for my clothing they cast lots. But you, LORD, do not stay far off; my strength, come quickly to help me. (Ps 22:17–20)

If she hadn't known it before, I suppose that, at that moment, Mary would have realized the Psalm was about her Son. I wonder if she repeated that last verse to herself—*But you,* LORD, *do not stay far off; my strength, come quickly to help me*—as a kind of mantra to calm herself. Certainly she didn't like what was going on, and maybe she was finding it difficult to resist grabbing the tunic away from the soldiers; but she knew it was part of God's plan, that somehow it was necessary.

Bike Theft

My only experience that even comes close to Mary's was the day our son's bicycle was stolen. It was tucked away in our garage—or so we thought—until Matt went out to get it for a bike ride. It was gone. We searched the yard, the street, and the alley and didn't find a trace. We knew only that it had been there at about the same time the day before.

We called the police. When the officer arrived, he took down all the information and then informed us that there'd recently been a streak of bicycle thefts in the neighborhood. He asked us to keep our eyes open and call the police department if we noticed anything fishy.

"Don't give up hope," he consoled. "These troublemakers usually heist a bike, take a joyride on it, and then abandon it somewhere. Most stolen bikes turn up eventually."

I wasn't much consoled. In fact, I was furious. We'd moved to this neighborhood because the old one was getting rough and we'd feared becoming victims of crime. Moving to this area allowed our kids to play and move about in freedom and safety. And now this! Even more, I was outraged that someone would so much as touch my child's property. How *dare* they? I had visions of catching the thieves and wringing their necks. The bike did turn up—more than a year later. The tires were almost threadbare, and the weather had completely washed away its color. It had been brilliant-neon burnt orange. Now it was a freaky, vomity pink. Yes, it was still rideable, but I was still miffed.

When I compare my reaction to the theft of Matt's bike to Mary's reaction to the taking of Jesus' tunic, I'm embarrassed and even ashamed. That was just a bicycle and, in the broad scope of things, nothing of real value. Yet I was mad as a hornet. What's more, I don't recall having reminded myself that there was a reason the bike had been stolen, that it was part of God's plan. I'm sure I knew it subconsciously, but I didn't do anything to make it surface. I hadn't approached it in faith, the way Mary had approached the casting of lots over Jesus' tunic in faith.

The Lioness

Does the furious lioness in you raise her angry paws whenever she senses her children have been treated unjustly? It can be difficult to maintain self-control then, especially when your maternal instincts are going wild. I remember attending a homeschool gathering and seeing one mother shouting at another mother. Her son had come crying to her with a bump on his head and pointing to the other mom's son. Instinctively, the first mom lashed out before she discovered what really happened. The bump on his head had come from the impact of being thrown backward and into the tree behind him after he had hit the other boy. It's so easy to fly off the handle, isn't it? Try taking a deep breath before acting, thinking about how Mary acted in faith when her Son was mistreated, and keeping in mind that there's a reason for everything. You might even want to make Mary's mantra your own: *But you,* Lord, *do not stay far off; my strength, come quickly to help me.*

Exhaustion

Mary must have been absolutely exhausted as she stood at the foot of the Cross. She would have been physically exhausted; she couldn't have had anything to eat or drink since the previous day. Likely, she hadn't slept the night before, either. How could she think of anyone but Jesus? She would have been mentally exhausted; it couldn't have been easy to take in all that was happening and to make sense of it. She would have been emotionally exhausted; could anyone count the tears that she had shed, the anguished sobs that had escaped her throat? Was she spiritually exhausted? Again, the words of Simeon come to mind, "and you yourself a sword will pierce," as the sword was thrust deeper and deeper into Mary's heart.

Think of the last time you were completely exhausted—physically, mentally, emotionally, and spiritually. How did that affect your ability to handle things? How did that affect your ability to take things in and sort them out? How did it affect the way you conducted yourself—your thoughts, moods, reactions, and responses? Perhaps the next time you find yourself in the throes of exhaustion, you can think of Mary at the foot of the Cross and ask her to help you endure.

The Grieving Mother-Child

It's all too easy to become focused on the idea of Mary as Jesus' Mother. However, it's equally important to consider her in light of her daughterhood. She is indeed a daughter of God just as much as she is the Mother of God. Hence, this curious title, "The Grieving Mother-Child," which reflects the essence of Mary's character. She was first of all a child of God. Pure and holy, wanting only his will in all things, she was innocently faithful to him. Mary was—and still is—the perfect child of the heavenly Father. As that perfect child, she would have wanted the crucifixion. She would have actually *wanted* it, because it was God's will, and because it was the only way to redeem mankind. The child of God in Mary would have wanted eternity for all children of God.

Mary also was a mother. Loving and devoted, she lived her whole life for her Son. There was nothing she wouldn't do for him, endure for him, give to him. At the foot of the Cross, she saw the Redeemer of mankind, but she also saw her desecrated, emaciated, crucified Son. The child she had given birth to and for whom she had spent her entire life caring, protecting, nurturing, and encouraging had been tortured as a common criminal and was now minutes from death. The mother in Mary would have wanted comfort for her Son.

Bittersweet Request

Mary was, then, both mother and child beneath the Cross. And at that moment, Jesus made one last, bittersweet request of his Mother: *When Jesus saw his mother and the disciple there whom he loved, he said to his mother, "Woman, behold, your son." Then he said to the disciple, "Behold, your mother." And from that hour the disciple took her into his home.* As Catholics we understand the disciple to represent all people, and therefore Jesus' instructions that the disciple care for Mary applies to all of us. From the Cross, Jesus asked Mary to let go of him (humanly speaking) and accept all of mankind as her children. So, the *Catechism of the Catholic Church* refers to Mary as being "a mother to us in the order of grace," meaning that she is truly our Mother but without having given physical birth to us.[3] Mary's heart was a genuine mother's heart. Can you imagine what that request meant for her? She had to say goodbye to her Son in the form she had known him for thirty-three years, with his irresistible smile, his gleaming eyes, his soothing voice. What mother wouldn't feel her heart tearing in two as she watched her child die? On the other hand, Mary was to become the Mother of a new family—the family of God. What mother wouldn't feel her heart burst with joy at the gift of being given more children? I can see how letting go of her Son, and at the same time accepting so many more children into her heart, would have been a bittersweet moment for Mary.

The Value of Suffering

All of the torment, pain, and anguish that Mary had braved had a meaning and purpose that was confirmed at the foot of the Cross. In faith Mary had witnessed Jesus' trial, scourging, crowning with thorns, carrying of the Cross, disrobing, crucifixion, and death. In faith she believed that it was not only necessary, but a beautiful part of God's plan. In faith she surrendered her heart to the sword predestined to pierce it.

Blessed Pope John Paul II saw Mary's suffering as meaningful, too, and wrote about it in his apostolic letter on redemptive suffering, *Salvifici Doloris*:

> And again, after the events of her Son's hidden and public life, events which she must have shared with acute sensitivity, it was on Calvary that Mary's suffering, beside the suffering of Jesus, reached an intensity which can hardly be imagined from a human point of view but which was mysterious and supernaturally fruitful for the redemption of the world. Her ascent of Calvary and her standing at the foot of the Cross together with the Beloved Disciple were a special sort of sharing in the redeeming death of her Son. And the words which she heard from his lips were a kind of solemn handing-over of this Gospel of suffering so that it could be proclaimed to the whole community of believers.[4]

A Woman of Profound Faith

Mary was the first to really understand redemptive suffering, and she offered it willingly, totally, unconditionally, and faithfully for the sake of our salvation. I think suffering is one of—if not *the*—hardest concepts for human beings to grapple with. We can barely make any sense out of it at all. Yet for Mary, suffering was truth. Her Son suffered so that man could be redeemed. She suffered as his helpmate in the plan of salvation and for love of God and of us. For Mary, suffering was a given.

Of course, that doesn't mean that Mary was a glutton for punishment! She didn't go around looking for new ways to inflict pain upon herself or others. It means that she accepted in faith both the pleasant and unpleasant moments of life, embracing them as symbols of God's love. Jumping for joy might seem like a ridiculous prospect when a child is down with a life-threatening infection or the home mortgage is foreclosed upon, and it would be for someone without faith like Mary's. But for those who strive to imitate Mary's faith, it's not so far out.

Mary could be content in suffering because her will coincided perfectly with God's. It might still have been tough to withstand, but even in the toughest of times she could surrender any aversion to suffering by resting in the arms of the heavenly Father as his beloved child. Mary new that, no matter what, God would provide her with the grace and guidance necessary to see it through. By her example, Mary shows us how we, too, can faithfully embrace suffering because of its vital role in redemption. That's because Mary is a woman of *profound faith*.

Enriching Our Motherhood

Thoughts to Ponder

So also the Blessed Virgin advanced in her pilgrimage of faith, and faithfully bore her union with her Son even to the cross, where, in accord with the divine plan, she stood, vehemently grieved with her Only-Begotten, and joined herself to his Sacrifice with a motherly heart, lovingly consenting to the immolation of the victim born of her.

In conceiving Christ, in giving birth to him, in feeding him, in presenting him to the Father in the Temple, in

suffering with him, as he died on the cross, she cooperated
in the work of the Savior in an altogether singular way, by
obedience, faith, hope and burning love, to restore super-
natural life to souls.

~Pope Paul VI, *Lumen Gentium*
November 21, 1964, 58, 61

Deepening Our Motherhood

....

Reflection and Application

- What most impressed you about the foot of the Cross narrative? Why?

- Have you or anyone in your family ever been falsely accused? What happened? How did you handle it?

- Have you or anyone in your family ever been the victim of theft or vandalism? What happened? How did you handle it?

- What provokes the lioness in you?

- How do you deal with exhaustion?

- Have you ever received a bittersweet request? What was it? How did you react?

Becoming the Grieving Mother-Child

··

Imitating Mary's Faith

1. Tame the lioness with practice, patience, and prayer.

2. Remember Mary's distress on Calvary when your children face seemingly insurmountable obstacles.

3. Keep in mind: There's no way out but through.

4. Strive to see suffering as a valuable part of God's plan.

5. Be aware of how you act and react when you are exhausted.

6. Believe there is meaning and purpose in even the most dire of circumstances.

7. Ask Mary to help you become a woman of profound faith.

Chapter 10

The
Disciple
Mother

Imitating Mary's Joy

Then they returned to Jerusalem from the mount called Olivet, which is near Jerusalem, a sabbath day's journey away. When they entered the city they went up to the upper room where they were staying, Peter and John and James and Andrew, Philip and Thomas, Bartholomew and Matthew, James son of Alphaeus, Simon the Zealot, and Judas son of James.

All these devoted themselves with one accord to prayer, together with some women, and Mary the mother of Jesus, and his brothers.

Acts 1:12–14

When the time for Pentecost was fulfilled, they were all in one place together. And suddenly there came from the sky a noise like a strong driving wind, and it filled the entire house in which they were.

Then there appeared to them tongues as of fire, which parted and came to rest on each one of them. And they were all filled with the holy Spirit and began to speak in different tongues, as the Spirit enabled them to proclaim.

Now there were devout Jews from every nation under heaven staying in Jerusalem. At this sound, they gathered in a large crowd, but they were confused because each one heard them speaking in his own language. They were astounded, and in amazement they asked, "Are not all these people who are speaking Galileans? Then how does each of us hear them in his own native language? We are Parthians, Medes, and Elamites, inhabitants of Mesopotamia, Judea and Cappadocia, Pontus and Asia, Phrygia and Pamphylia, Egypt and the districts of Libya near Cyrene, as well as travelers from Rome, both Jews and converts to Judaism, Cretans and Arabians, yet we hear them speaking in our own tongues of the mighty acts of God."

They were all astounded and bewildered, and said to one another, "What does this mean?"

But others said, scoffing, "They have had too much new wine."

Then Peter stood up with the Eleven, raised his voice, and proclaimed to them, "You who are Jews, indeed all of you staying in Jerusalem. Let this be known to you, and listen to my words.

"These people are not drunk, as you suppose, for it is only nine o'clock in the morning. No, this is what was spoken through the prophet Joel:

'It will come to pass in the last days,' God says, 'that I will pour out a portion of my spirit upon all flesh. Your sons and your daughters shall prophesy, your young men shall see visions, your old men shall dream dreams. Indeed, upon my servants and my handmaids I will pour out a portion of my spirit in those days, and they shall prophesy. And I will work wonders in the heavens above and signs on the earth below: blood, fire, and a cloud of smoke. The sun shall be turned to darkness, and the moon to blood, before the coming of the great and splendid day of the Lord, and it shall be that everyone shall be saved who calls on the name of the Lord.'"

Acts 2:1–21

What an awesome scene! In the Pentecost narrative, we see a number of firsts. Among them is the Church's first novena, instituted by Jesus Christ himself when he instructed his apostles to return to Jerusalem and await the coming of the Paraclete. From this developed the novena in honor of the Holy Spirit, which is the only novena officially prescribed by the Church.[1] For that reason, I love novenas, even though I have a dickens of a time keeping up with them once I get started. Any time I pray a novena, I can't help but remember Mary, there with the apostles in the upper room and united in prayer for nine days. It gives me goosebumps to think about the experience that would be.

New Births

Also in the scene, we see Mary again joined with the Holy Spirit in a new birth. At the Annunciation, she was overshadowed by the Spirit, and consequently conceived our Lord in her womb. At Pentecost, she was overshadowed by the Holy Spirit and conceived, so to speak, the nascent Church. From the Annunciation to Pentecost, Mary was led by the Holy Spirit, always in tune with the heavenly Father's will, always in perfect surrender to him. Thus, at Pentecost she is revealed as the "new Eve," the Woman who would untie the knot that Adam and Eve tied. The *Catechism* describes it this way: "At the end of this mission of the Spirit, Mary became the Woman, the new Eve ('mother of the living'), the mother of the 'whole Christ.' As such, she was present with the Twelve, who 'with one accord devoted themselves to prayer,' at the dawn of the 'end time' which the Spirit was to inaugurate on the morning of Pentecost with the manifestation of the Church."[2]

Mary's mission was not only to physically give birth to Jesus, but also to spiritually give birth to the Church by cooperating in God's plan for our salvation. "After her Son's Ascension, Mary 'aided the beginnings of the Church by her prayers.' In her association with the apostles and several women, 'we also see Mary by her prayers imploring the gift of the Spirit, who had already overshadowed her in the Annunciation.'"[3]

Famous Paintings

Famous paintings of Pentecost (and even not-so-famous ones) tend to depict the event as much smaller than it actually was. If Mary is included in the paintings at all, she is usually the only woman, surrounded by twelve men (the apostles). It certainly is a beautiful image, and I'm sure that there was a special closeness between the apostles and Mary. After all, she was the Mother of their Lord, their friend, the man they loved with all their hearts. We tend to forget that it wasn't just Mary and the apostles present in the upper room; there were 120 people in a mixed group of men and women (Acts 1:15).

It's assumed that at least some of the women in the upper room were the same ones who stood with Mary at the foot of the Cross, and also the same ones who accompanied Jesus' body to the tomb and received the message of the Resurrection from the angel. This is an important message for us, and especially for women who think that women are discriminated against by the Church. For, according to the scripture passage, the women were obviously an integral part of the group awaiting the coming of the Spirit. It didn't stop there, of course, because they also were among those who entered the streets to preach the Good News.

In the Midst of It All

And there was Mary, in the midst of all of this. I find it remarkable that, even though she was the mother of Jesus—a very important figure in the early Church—she didn't do anything to make herself stand out from the others gathered there. She was positioned as one of the members of the whole group, in the presence of the Spirit, and eager to share God's light with the world. In fact, scripture doesn't even quote her, although she surely would have spoken to the others. How can you be part of a group for nine days and not enter into conversation?

I wonder what that was like for Mary. Had she been able to recuperate from her exhaustion at the crucifixion? Was she able to find nourishment and regain her strength? Had she spent time silently, prayerfully reviewing all that had happened and pondering the fulfillment of God's promise to her people? Was she starting to miss Jesus, or was she utterly filled with joy over the Resurrection? I have a feeling it was both.

Saying Goodbye

Monica moved out of the house when she was nineteen years old. It nearly killed me to see her go, even though she moved in with some wonderful Catholic women, was only ten minutes from home, and I saw her often because we were working in the same apostolate together. Still, it didn't matter. Around the house, I intensely felt her absence. Around every corner, I was somehow reminded that she wasn't there anymore. Since Monica is our only daughter, I was left to live as the sole woman among three males—Mark and our sons Luke and John. Matt had already moved out by that time. My well-meaning menfolk tried to console me by calling to my attention the fact that our dog is female, and wasn't that almost as good as having another woman around? Nice try.

For as much as I missed her, I was overjoyed at Monica's opportunity to strike out on her own in a holy and safe environment. I was also elated at all of the new opportunities that were before her—school, work, new friends, independence. She was in a great place and had great things ahead of her. So, in spite of the painful twinge in my heart, there also was a vast amount of joy. I can imagine that it was like this for Mary, only her joy would have been so much more profound! Jesus was in the greatest place of all, with the greatest things ahead of him.

I'm sure you've felt that way at times, haven't you? Your children may not be grown and moved out of the house, but you still can understand what it's like to miss them when they're not around, and yet be joyful that they're involved in something wonderful and fruitful. Is it like that when they go away to summer camp? To school? To the seminary or convent? What about a pilgrimage or a pro-life rally? All of these things can evoke the same kind of response in us that Mary had.

I Know You

How does one even begin to imagine the descent of the Holy Spirit? A mighty wind, tongues of fire, and the miracle of speaking in tongues—there is no comparison to these in our everyday experiences. How would it be to not only sense the presence of the Holy Spirit but to be completely enveloped in him—really him? I don't know that there is anything else, aside from receiving our Lord in the Eucharist, that could elicit a joy that profound. And Mary was there, taking it all in among the others. I wonder sometimes if, when the Holy Spirit descended in the upper room, Mary recognized him—not through the wind and fire, nor even the tongues—but because she had been so intimately touched by him at the Annunciation. Did that, too, give her joy?

I also can't help but ponder what it was like for Mary to hear the apostles suddenly speaking in a variety of languages that, clearly, none of them had known before. Did she think she was hearing things? Had she gone mad? Perhaps she thought she was still exhausted from the crucifixion. Was it a wild, practical joke? Of course not, but I can imagine that Mary could have been baffled by what she was hearing and observing.

More Than Just Gibberish

When John was small, he had a favorite game that still makes us all chuckle. I still have my old Smith Corona typewriter, the one I wrote my very first article on—yeah, I know that makes me akin to the dinosaurs—nonetheless, it was a novelty to the kids, since they grew up in the computer age. I remember getting out the typewriter, sitting it on the dining room table, and letting John type away to his heart's content. It took quite awhile sometimes for that little heart to be content! When finished, he would bring his "story" to me and have me read it. This was before he could read and write, so there really weren't any words, just a string of letters mixed with spaces. I'd look very serious, as if I was about to read an important document, and then I would proceed to pronounce (as best I could) John's "words." You can suppose that it sounded like a crazy bunch of gibberish, and it was. However, it got us laughing uproariously because it sounded so funny. John liked to pretend that he had made up a new language and written a story for me in it. What I like most about that memory is the joy that bubbled up inside of us as we fooled around with the typewriter, and the joy that still erupts when we think back to those happy times.

Do you have a memory like that? Is there something from your family's past that made joy simply bubble up within you at the time, and still does now? When that happens, you can think of Mary looking around, hearing all the absurd words and bubbling over with joy at recognizing the Holy Spirit at work in the upper room. When you have joyous times like that in your family, the Holy Spirit is at work in your home.

A Proud Mother

Can you imagine how proud Mary was of Peter when he stepped out into the streets to proclaim the Gospel? Peter must have been like a son to her, not only because she was his Mother in the order of grace, but also because he was one of her Son's closest friends. I think she would have been joyously proud! Peter, "scaredy-cat Peter," who had denied our Lord three times, walked out into public and "raised his voice, and proclaimed to them":

> You who are Jews, indeed all of you staying in Jerusalem. Let this be known to you, and listen to my words.
>
> These people are not drunk, as you suppose, for it is only nine o'clock in the morning. No, this is what was spoken through the prophet Joel:
>
> "It will come to pass in the last days," God says, "that I will pour out a portion of my spirit upon all flesh. Your sons and your daughters shall prophesy, your young men shall see visions, your old men shall dream dreams. Indeed, upon my servants and my handmaids I will pour out a

portion of my spirit in those days, and they shall prophesy. And I will work wonders in the heavens above and signs on the earth below: blood, fire, and a cloud of smoke. The sun shall be turned to darkness, and the moon to blood, before the coming of the great and splendid day of the Lord, and it shall be that everyone shall be saved who calls on the name of the Lord." (Acts 2:14–21)

Peter didn't go quietly from person to person. No, he stood strong in the crowd and shouted his proclamation. Keep in mind that the folks in the upper room were filled with joy, but the folks on the streets were filled with skepticism, even hatred for Jesus and his followers. They wouldn't all have been excited to hear the Good News; some would've wanted to crucify the apostles as they did Jesus. What Peter did took guts, and I can see how it would have delighted Mary. Is there a chance she even cheered him on?

The Floodgates

My kids laugh at me, and I think sometimes are a little annoyed with me, because I cry at important events. Well, I don't just cry—I sob uncontrollably, pathetically, and it can be downright embarrassing for them. There's something about seeing my kids recognized or receiving an honor of some kind that rips open the floodgates. I'm liable to send the entire population floating away when they receive the sacraments. When John was preparing to be confirmed, he warned me—not once, but several times—that I'd better not embarrass him at his Confirmation.

"You're kidding me, right?" I exclaimed. "Okay, fine. I'll do my best."

"No," John replied. "Do better than your best." I sighed.

On the day of John's Confirmation, I tried to keep busy in order to distract myself from the emotions that I knew were building up inside me. As we were getting ready to go to the church, I considered whether or not I should bring tissues.

"Naw," I told myself, "I'll be fine. I'm not going to cry." I almost believed myself.

The *confirmande* had to be there an hour before, so John and Mark left early, and I stayed behind so I could find a seat with the rest of the clan.

As they walked out the door, John turned to me, gave me a stern stare, and said, *"Don't. You. Dare."*

After they'd gone, I felt that old familiar lump in my throat, but I fought back the tears. "I'll be fine," I kept telling myself.

When it was time for me to leave, I grabbed my purse and the camera and headed for the door. I put my hand on the door handle, took a deep breath, and . . . the flood started. I shook my head, "I can't!" I turned around, scurried into the bathroom, and stuffed my purse with packs of tissue.

At the church, I tried to gather my composure, and actually did a pretty good job of it—until, that is, I looked behind me and caught a glimpse of the *confirmande* lining up in the vestibule. That did it. I lost all control, and sobbed through the entire entrance procession.

"Holy mackerel!" Matt marveled when he looked over and saw the downpour.

Luke, sitting on the other side of me, raised his eyebrows, looked over, and said, "You're kidding me!"

Nope. I wasn't kidding. I did everything in my power to get a grip on myself, and I did, for a while, until it was time for John to be confirmed. I couldn't see him, but I could see the back of the head of his sponsor, and that's all it took. The floodgates flew open again. Matt reached over and gave me a supportive hug, letting me know that the clan loves me just the way I am—sobbing and all. I've always been inclined to cry at happy events, even at the weddings, Baptisms, First Communions, and Confirmations of people I don't even know. When it's one of my kids? Look out! Joyful things just make me overflow with emotion.

Daring the Truth

I can see how, at Pentecost, Mary would've been proud of, not only Peter, but all of the followers of Jesus who dared to bring the truth to the rest of the world. Did she get choked up when she heard someone telling of Jesus' crucifixion and the promise of the Resurrection? Maybe she carried a handkerchief around with her in order to catch the tears. Did her heart swell with joy upon seeing the new believers baptized? She was probably ecstatic every time a community of Christians was formed.

The Most Perfect Disciple

There also is another dimension to this—a very personal one between Jesus and Mary—that would have brought Mary great joy. Mary was the first and most perfect disciple of Jesus. She loved God; she loved all of God's children; and she wanted more than anything for them to enjoy the happiness of heaven.

She understood that all that was happening before her was part of the unfolding of God's plan for mankind's salvation: *And it shall be that everyone shall be saved who calls on the name of the Lord . . . .* That alone would have filled her with joy. But remember that Mary was also witnessing the culmination of Jesus' mission here on earth. She had been part of his life for thirty-three years. She had given birth to him, nurtured, protected, educated, consoled, and encouraged him. She had eaten, drunk, prayed, and played with him. She had raised and guided him during his life with the Holy Family and then walked along with him in his public ministry. Their lives, their fates, were intertwined. His mission was her mission. She had seen him struggle, weep, succeed, laugh, and work to bring God's kingdom to their people. She had watched him suffer excruciatingly and die for that kingdom. And now that kingdom, for which her Son had spent every last drop of his human strength—even to the point of shedding his blood—was flourishing right before her eyes. Can you imagine what that was like for Mary?

Clothed in the Sun

One of my favorite images of Mary is from the book of Revelation, but it is related to the Pentecost narrative, at least in my mind. It is the "woman clothed with the sun":

> Then God's temple in heaven was opened, and the ark of his covenant could be seen in the temple. There were flashes of lightning, rumblings, and peals of thunder, an earthquake, and a violent hailstorm. A great sign appeared

in the sky, a woman clothed with the sun, with the moon
under her feet, and on her head a crown of twelve stars.
(Rv 11:19, 12:1)

The woman described in Revelation 12 primarily symbolizes
the People of God, Israel, and the Church. However, there is
strong evidence—although not definitive—that indicates she
also represents Mary.[4] Regardless, this passage conjures up a
picture of Mary for me. The reason I especially love this image
is because it enables me to imagine the extreme joy that Mary
must have felt at the Resurrection.

Once, in an Easter homily, the priest described how he
imagined the moment of the Resurrection. He was convinced
that Jesus had to have appeared first to his Mother upon ris-
ing from the dead, since he loved her so very much. He even
suggested that Jesus may have found her sleeping, entered her
room quietly, and gently kissed her cheek in order to awaken
and surprise her. How lovely!

Celebrating Victory

I've always thought that same thing, and so for me, the woman
clothed with the sun symbolizes Mary's celebration of our
Lord's victory over Satan. I can just see her, thrilled beyond
compare, in all her majestic beauty, rejoicing with Jesus, "We
did it! We did it!"

Perhaps we, too, can be women "clothed with the sun,"
when our husbands and children achieve victory. That's easy
to do when it's something big; it's not as easy to do when
it's something barely noticeable. Our families count on us

for moral support and look to us for approval. We can be so busy, preoccupied, overworked, or distracted that we miss their accomplishments. No matter the size, we're needed to acknowledge every success and spread the joy. Like Mary, we should feel proud of them and thrilled beyond compare, rejoicing with them, "You did it! You did it!"

A Woman of Profound Joy

Whether we think of Mary as a simple, Jewish mother or the woman clothed with the sun, we can try to feel her joy and make it our own, for our family's sake and our own. We can think of all the moments in Mary's life that would have brought her joy. Did she laugh and clap her hands when Jesus took his first step? Did she good-naturedly gloat to the other mothers when he learned his first scripture passage? What about the day he copied the Hebrew alphabet without any help? Did she marvel when he completed his first woodworking project? Perhaps it was a table, which Mary quickly set for a meal so that the Holy Family could appreciate Jesus' handiwork together. We daily have moments like these in our own families; we need only open our eyes to them and allow ourselves to appreciate them.

The challenge for us—as it may have been for Mary—is to foster joy in such a way that it prevails even during the dark times of our lives. Moodiness, physical changes, and emotional and spiritual obstacles all can weigh us down and tempt us away from joyfulness. We can't avoid these perils, but we can prevent downfalls by taking time regularly—daily if possible, and hourly if necessary—to contemplate Mary's joy, searching for ways to understand and imitate it.

There is much in the Pentecost narrative to take in, digest, and apply. In so many ways, Mary had reason to be joyful, and I have no doubt that she radiated that joy to everyone around her. I believe that Mary had a special "Pentecost joy," long before the nine days in the upper room. By this, I don't mean to imply that Mary could see into the future. She was human as we are, so she would not have had that gift. Rather, I mean that Mary's total devotion to God would have prompted her to be joyful simply in knowing that she, and all of humanity, rested in God's hands. The scriptures promised a Redeemer; that would have been enough to permanently fill her heart with joy. That's because Mary is a woman of *profound joy*.

Enriching Our Motherhood

Thoughts to Ponder

By reason of the gift and role of divine maternity, by which she is united with her Son, the Redeemer, and with his singular graces and functions, the Blessed Virgin is also intimately united with the Church. As St. Ambrose taught, the Mother of God is a type of the Church in the order of faith, charity and perfect union with Christ. For in the mystery of the Church, which is itself rightly called mother and virgin, the Blessed Virgin stands out in eminent and singular fashion as exemplar both of virgin and mother. By her belief and obedience, not knowing man but overshadowed by the Holy Spirit, as the new Eve she brought forth on earth the very Son of the Father, showing an undefiled faith, not in the word of the ancient serpent, but in that of God's messenger. The Son whom she brought forth is he whom God placed as the first-born among many brethren, namely the faithful, in whose birth and education she cooperates with a maternal love.

~Pope Paul VI, *Lumen Gentium*, November 21, 1964, 63.

Deepening Our Motherhood

Reflection and Application

- What most impressed you about the Pentecost narrative?
- How do you express joy?
- Have you ever deeply missed one of your children? When? What was that like?
- What is your most joyful family memory? Describe it.
- How do you celebrate your husband and children's accomplishments?

Becoming the Disciple Mother

Imitating Mary's Joy

1. Appreciate your value as a woman in the Church.
2. Foster joyful family memories.
3. Celebrate your family's accomplishments and special events (especially the sacraments!).

4. Be genuinely proud of your family—and show it.

5. Strive to become a woman clothed with the sun.

6. Ask Mary to help you be a woman of profound joy.

Letting *Mary* Mother Us

Lord,
Grant that we may receive
the effect of the offering we dedicate to you,
so that, walking with the Blessed Virgin Mary in the way
    of beauty,
we may be renewed in progress in the life of the Spirit
and at last to the vision of your glory.
We ask this through Christ our Lord.

Prayer over the Gifts[1]

At the Prayer over the Gifts of every Mass I attend, I place my own special offering on the paten along with the hosts. Usually, my offering includes the trials, defeats, and burdens I've had to suffer, but also the gifts I've been given and the victories, milestones, and achievements I've experienced during the

157

week. Always, my offering includes whatever I've given to, and received from, my family—I lay it all there on the paten, and I ask the heavenly Father to bless and accept my imperfect sacrifice along with the perfect sacrifice of his Son. When the priest lifts the paten at the Consecration, I imagine my sacrifice being lifted up to heaven and placed into God the Father's hands. I want all that I am, think, say, and do as a wife and mother to be made holy and acceptable to God.

A Familiar Face

What's more, I picture Mary standing beside the priest at the altar. She spent her entire life in devotion to her Son, exemplifying the virtues of patience, trust, obedience, endurance, courage, strength, hope, faith, and joy in every moment. Why would she *not* want to be present at every holy Mass, close to her Son, participating and rejoicing in the fulfillment of his mission? She was, is, and always will be a loving mother to Jesus, and to us. How could she not want to place all that she experiences as our Mother on the paten with the hosts, offering them as sacrifice to the heavenly Father? I don't simply imagine that she's there; I allow my mind's eye to really "see" her, to envision her beauty, reverence, love, and profound adoration. There is a particular image of Mary with which I grew up. It's called "Mother Thrice Admirable, Queen and Victress of Schoenstatt," thus named because the Apostolic Movement of Schoenstatt enthrones this image in all of their Marian shrines throughout the world. I've become so accustomed to Mary's face that I can bring her to life, so to speak, in just about any circumstance.

Perhaps this is something that you can do, too. Find an image that you particularly like—it doesn't have to be the Schoenstatt image—and meditate on it, taking it deeply into your mind and heart. Become accustomed to Mary's face so that you can bring her to life in just about any circumstance. The more you can "see" her, the more you'll get to know her, the more you'll open your heart to her, and the deeper you'll come to love her and her Son. She wants to be your Mother, and she's hoping that you want to be her child so that you can walk with her in the way of beauty and be renewed in progress in the life of the Spirit.

Mary's Motherly Duties

At the foot of the Cross, Mary was given special duties that she takes very seriously. Pope Leo XIII wrote in his encyclical, *Octobri Mense*, "In the person of his disciple John, Christ entrusted the entire human race to the loving care of his Mother. . . . With a generous heart she embraced the heritage of the enormous labors which her dying Son left to her, and she immediately began to fulfill all her duties towards us all."[2]

Mary's Motherly Rights

Mary loves us as deeply as any mother could, and she wants to help us become genuine, virtuous mothers like herself. Opening our hearts and minds to her is the first step; getting to know her by studying her life (the ten climaxes and virtues in this book) is the second step. The third step is allowing her to transform us. We can begin doing that by giving her motherly rights over us. If that sounds a bit oppressive to you, try thinking of it in terms of the word "surrender." Giving her rights over us means to be receptive, willing, and open to her ability to change and educate us. How does Mary educate us? First, of course, she educates us through her example, but also by guiding us through the various circumstances and situations from which we can learn. Sometimes that will take us to the heights of bliss; at other times, it will hurt, but the pain will be worth it. We'll be understanding more about ourselves and growing in virtue.

Oh, Mom!

If you hang around my home long enough, you'll catch me mumbling something like, "Oh, Mom! What on earth is going on?" or, "Seriously, Mom!" Initially, the kids thought I was talking to myself and wondered if I had a loose screw. I didn't, and I still don't (at least I don't think so). I was actually talking to Mary, wondering about something or other that I couldn't figure out. It might have been an article that I just couldn't fit together. Maybe someone said or did something to me that I couldn't understand. Or, perhaps I was troubled over a child's dilemma. It might simply have been frustration over my own limitations. No matter—the point is that when I get "stuck," I turn to Mary, looking for guidance just like any daughter would from her mother. I call her "Mom," not out of disrespect, but rather because she's so real to me, and I sense that she's interested in every tiny detail of my life—just like she's interested in every tiny detail of your life.

Hints and Signs

Giving Mary rights over us also means being aware of every sign that she gives us, every hint she sends, and all of the ways in which she will ask us to be instruments of virtue. As any good mother, Mary will try to grab our attention when we're about to falter, redirect us when we've turned the wrong way, or encourage us when we're on the right path. Her ways are subtle; but, if we are alert, we will notice when she's "talking" to us.

When we were in the process of buying the house that we now live in, the city noticed that there were some code violations and therefore disallowed the sale of the property until the owner had fixed the violations. The owner agreed, and we thought that was that. A couple of days before the closing, we took a final walk through and saw that the code violations hadn't been touched. Not only that, but the owners—in anger over the ordinance—had caused further damage to the interior of the house. It was in bad shape.

Mark and I thought about it, prayed about it, and then decided to back out of the deal. Unfortunately, the real estate agent was about to go on vacation out of state and wasn't inclined to have anything get in the way. We had already sold our old house, and the vacating date was nonnegotiable. Either we bought the house, damage and all, or we wouldn't have a place to live in two days. With three young children and no backup resources, we were stuck. So, we placed the whole mess into Mary's hands and asked her to take charge. She did.

We still had to fix up the house, but we received untold blessings as a consequence of buying the property. The kids thrived, the neighborhood was great, Lake Michigan with its gorgeous shoreline was only six blocks away, the library was around the corner, the people were wonderful, and the city had an outstanding Fourth of July fireworks display along with a fantastic, small-town feel that just couldn't be beat. We really felt comfortable and at home; some of our most cherished family memories were spawned here. We are convinced that when we placed the situation into Mary's care, she interceded for us and saw to it that we got the hint, that is, the real estate agent's obstinacy. Had he not refused to help us, we would have looked for another property and missed out on all of the good things God had in store for us in our current location.

If you look carefully, you'll notice hints from Mary, too. They won't hit you over the head, at least not usually. They'll probably be subtle or even mysterious. I bet you've already experienced many in your life. Have you ever had an inexplicable inclination to do a kind deed for someone, and then later found out that the person had been feeling lonely or depressed? Have you ever had a premonition that one of your children was in danger? Perhaps you've been stuck in a quandary and then out of nowhere run across a book or article that gave you the answer. Maybe you've been in need of something that suddenly appeared through the hands of a friend or relative. All of these are ways in which Mary was sending you signs and hints, protecting you, nurturing you, guiding you, and inspiring you toward greater virtue.

The rights we give her allow Mary to put her "stamp" on our hearts. When we do that, we allow her to exercise three dimensions of her motherhood: her motherly power, her motherly kindness, and her motherly wisdom.

Mary's Motherly Power

It's not common to consider Mary as powerful—at least not in the same way that we imagine God's almighty power, which is evidenced by our Lord's conquering of death. Mary's power is different, as it is rooted in her place of honor beside her Son, as his permanent helpmate in his work of salvation. In this way, we could say that her most natural position is to help him pursue souls for eternity. Her power lies in her ability to defend those who invoke her when tempted by the devil. It is through her intercession that we can find great power to defeat the enemy, and as the Mother of God, her wishes and petitions are given special consideration. We see this symbolically represented at the wedding at Cana, when Jesus changed the water into wine for the wedding couple at his Mother's request.

That same maternity is extended to us. Mary longs to take care of us, to nurture us, to protect us, and to guide us in the same way she has loved her Son. When we open our hearts to her as our mother, and call on her in times of need, her power becomes obvious and irresistible.

Mary's Motherly Kindness

Mary's motherly kindness is most evident in the title given her by the Church, "Queen of Mercy." No one can fully grasp the length and breadth and height and depth of Mary's mercy. Because of her perfection—free from original sin and an unblemished instrument in God's hands—Mary's mercy closely reflects God's mercy. St. Alphonsus Liguori explains it this way: "It is, however, not to us with Mary, who, although a Queen, is not a Queen of justice, intent on the punishment of the wicked, but acquitted of mercy, intent only on commiserating with and pardoning sinners. And this is the reason for which the Church requires that we should expressly call her, 'Queen of Mercy.'"[3]

Of course, there are other ways—countless ways—in which Mary exercises her motherly kindness. Primarily, she wants our salvation; but beyond that she wants all the things that any good mother wants for her child. She wants our comfort, happiness, fruitfulness, wellness, prosperity, and holiness. She sees to it that we have these things, through her intercession, hints, and signs, always in accord with God's will.

Mary's Motherly Wisdom

Mary's motherly wisdom is most evident in the title given her by the Church, "Seat of Wisdom." Mary not only represents the interests of man before God through her intercessory power, but she also represents God's wishes before mankind. In other words, she helps us to discern and follow God's will. True Christian wisdom is love for the Cross and the Crucified. And so Mary, in her motherly wisdom, helps us to love the Cross and the Crucified as she loves them herself.

She doesn't merely guide us toward the Cross; she directs us toward all that is holy and pleasing to God. As the *Catechism* states,

> Mary, the all-holy ever-virgin Mother of God, is the masterwork of the mission of the Son and the Spirit in the fullness of time. For the first time in the plan of salvation and because his Spirit had prepared her, the Father found the

dwelling place where his Son and his Spirit could dwell among men. In this sense the Church's Tradition has often read the most beautiful texts on wisdom in relation to Mary. Mary is acclaimed and represented in the liturgy as the "Seat of Wisdom." In her, the "wonders of God" that the Spirit was to fulfill in Christ and the Church began to be manifested.[4]

Your Motherly Power

You, too, can exercise motherly power, kindness, and mercy, although not in the same way that Mary does. You have the power of intercession for your husband and children before God (and certainly before Mary). Your motherly prayers, especially when your children are grown, will do more for your children than anything you could ever physically do for them. In fact, at times you'll find that praying is the *only* thing you can do for them! You have power to protect your family from the devil by creating a holy atmosphere in your home, helping them to participate frequently in the sacraments, making way for daily prayer, and placing them again and again in Mary's care.

Your Motherly Kindness

You can, of course, demonstrate motherly kindness through deeds of love for your family—the housekeeping, cooking, chauffeuring, and all the "extras" that you do for them. But you also can exhibit motherly kindness by becoming, so to speak, a "queen of mercy." Show mercy to your husband and children; be forgiving of their faults and infractions. Don't be too proud to ask their mercy and forgiveness for your own faults and infractions. Help them to be merciful and forgiving toward each other.

Your Motherly Wisdom

Finally, you manifest your motherly wisdom by seeking Mary's counsel in all things and then leading your husband and children to do the same. Don't be afraid to share with your kids the times when you are confused, worried, or unsure. It's been my experience that hiding these things actually does more harm than good in the long run. Kids need to see their parents struggle sometimes so that they can learn how to work through their own struggles, particularly when they reach adulthood. Talk about it, pray about it, together when possible. Your example of patiently, trustfully, faithfully, and prayerfully working through the joys, sorrows, and mires of your life will help your kids to do the same.

Walking in the Way of Mary's Beauty

All that we have learned about Mary in *Imitating Mary*— her life, her virtues, and her motherly power, kindness, and mercy—helps us to walk in the way of her beauty. When we recall the scenes in Mary's life, we can see her more fully as a real human mother who had the same experiences and emotions that we do. Studying them again and again will help us to develop an ever deepening relationship with Mary, not only in a divine way, but also in a solid, substantial way that feels natural and becomes part of our daily living. When we contemplate Mary's virtues, we cultivate a greater appreciation for her as a woman, as Mother of God, and as our Mother and foster an ever-increasing yearning to make Mary's virtues our own. When we strive for practical application of those virtues we become better women, wives, and mothers, which will bring blessings upon ourselves, our families, the Church, and the entire world.

That won't happen overnight. It takes a moment to conceive a child but a lifetime to figure out how to properly mother him. Sound like a discouraging statement? Well, it's not. I actually mean it to encourage you, because there's no possible way that you can know everything about being a mother without ever having been one! As your child grows, you will too. At each new stage of his life, you'll enter a new one of your own. Try your hardest, but leave room for mistakes and adjustments. Above all, trust that God will give you the grace you need to parent.

> By reason of their state in life and of their order, Christian spouses have their own special gifts in the People of God. This grace proper to the sacrament of Matrimony is intended to perfect the couple's love and to strengthen their indissoluble unity. By this grace they help one another to attain holiness in their married life and in welcoming and educating their children.[5]

You're a Better Mother than You Think You Are

Lastly, I want to encourage you by affirming that you're a better mother than you think you are. Mothers have an innate tendency toward self-criticism. We have the gift of long-suffering, and we sure do like to suffer long with ourselves, don't we? We also like to compare ourselves with other mothers, and that only makes things worse. You can't be that other mom; you can only be you, and you are *beautiful*—inside and out! Take time every single day to acknowledge something good about yourself—a deed you did, a quality you possess, or a problem you solved. Think often of the little signs of love that you've received from your family, and savor them. There are some women who believe they can't be good mothers if they've had a rough background or a negative experience of a mother while they were growing up. While those things do affect you, they needn't keep you from being a wonderful, loving, and capable mom. No obstacle will. Do you know why? Because you have the promise of God's grace and Mary as your Mother, educator, model, and guide.

Enriching Our Motherhood

Thoughts to Ponder

When we penetrate into the truths of this rich endowment which God has so abundantly given to the Mother of Christianity—motherly power, motherly kindness, and motherly wisdom—then we can see that she is capable of fulfilling her motherly task in a masterful way, her task of nourishing us with every kind of gift and grace, of educating us to be as perfect an image of Christ as possible for the glorification of the Father—that should reach the point where we can say, 'My life is Christ's life: the life I live now is not my own, is Christ living in me—and of leading us to victory as her instruments in her battle against the devil and the world, so that Christ's dominion be established on earth. With that it is no longer difficult for us to acknowledge her mother writes over us.

~Fr. Joseph Kentenich[6]

Deepening Our Motherhood

Reflection and Application

- Which of Mary's virtues stand out most for you? Why?
- What is your favorite image of Mary? Why?
- What do you do when you get "stuck" in a perplexing situation?
- Has there ever been a time when you sensed God or Mary's presence in your life? How did you know?
- In what ways can you show motherly power, kindness, and wisdom?

Imitating Mary's Power, Kindness, and Wisdom

1. Become familiar with Mary's face—find an image of her that you can "bring to life."
2. Meditate on Mary's life and virtues.

3. Look out for Mary's hints and signs.

4. Seek Mary's counsel in all things—and let your family
    observe you doing it.

5. Ask Mary to help you acquire her motherly power, kind-
    ness, and wisdom.

6. Remember that motherhood doesn't happen overnight.

7. Realize that you're a better mother than you think you
    are.

Acknowledgments

By far, this has been the most rewarding, and at the same time, the most difficult book I've ever written. It was clear all along that the evil one didn't want *Imitating Mary* published, and he tried in every way to stop it. Obviously, he failed. Once again, Mary was victorious as Queen of my heart, my work, and my life. Of course, she was helped by the many people who diligently prayed and sacrificed for me as I worked, and they deserve credit. This book wouldn't have made it without them!

Front and center is the Fenelon clan: First, my husband, Mark, who's been my right arm—and sometimes both of my arms—these past three decades. Then, our children, Matthew, Monica, Luke, and John who were hit with some of the aforementioned obstacles, and yet refused to be discouraged themselves nor to let me become discouraged. You guys amaze me! And, special thanks to John for doing piles upon piles of dishes so that I could have more time to work on the manuscript. What a trooper! Ever loving and ever supportive, the clan keeps me reaching ever higher toward the ideal of motherhood, our Mother Mary. I love you! Thank you!

My editor, Kristi McDonald, has been astounding in her advice and encouragement. Bob Hamma and the rest of the staff at Ave Maria Press have been phenomenal in welcoming me into the Ave Maria family and in their enthusiasm for my book, but also for me as an author. Thanks to all of you.

In the early stages of the manuscript, I received priceless feedback from Fr. Mark Niehaus, Elizabeth Grusenski, and Kendra Youren Valenzuela. They are intelligent, insightful, and generous people dedicated to this project. Thank you.

Finally, Fr. Jonathan Niehaus, I.S.P., my greatest advocate professionally, personally, and spiritually for nearly two decades, helped me unfold the concept for *Imitating Mary* before he lost his battle with cancer on January 19, 2012, and continues to intercede and guide me from heaven. Thank you, Father!

Notes

1. Mary's Fiat

1. Paul VI, *Lumen Gentium*, November 21, 1964, http://www.vatican.va/archive/hist_councils/ii_vatican_council/documents/vat-ii_const_19641121_lumen-gentium_en.html

2. The Unwed Mother

1. Elizabeth Johnson, *Truly Our Sister: A Theology of Mary in the Communion of Saints* (New York: The Continuum International Publishing Group, 2003), 190.

2. Ibid. 191.

3. The Handmaiden Mother

1. Leo XIII, *Octobri Mense*, September 22, 1891, http://www.vatican.va/holy_father/leo_xiii/encyclicals/documents/hf_l-xiii_enc_22091891_octobri-mense_en.html.

2. Joseph Kentenich, *Mary, Our Mother and Educator: An Applied Mariology*, trans. Jonathan Niehaus (Waukesha, WI: Schoenstatt Sisters of Mary, 1987), 85–86.

4. The Messenger Mother

1. "On the Road: The Inns and Outs of Travel in First-Century Palestine," *Christianity Today Library* accessed June 23, 2012, http://www.ctlibrary.com/ch/1998/issue59/59h028.html.

2. Raymond E. Brown, Karl P. Donfried, Joseph A. Fitzmyer, and John Reumann, eds., *Mary in the New Testament* (New York: Paulist Press, 1978), 139–40.

5. The Young Mother

1. Pope Benedict XVI, General Audience, December 28, 2011, http://www.vatican.va/holy_father/benedict_xvi/audiences/2011/documents/hf_ben-xvi_aud_20111228_en.html.

6. The Committed Mother

1. Paul VI, *Marialis Cultus*, February 2, 1974, http://www.vatican.va/holy_father/paul_vi/apost_exhortations/documents/hf_p-vi_exh_19740202_marialis-cultus_en.html.

2. Joseph Kentenich, "My Queen, My Mother," in *Heavenwards*, trans. Jonathan Niehaus (Waukesha, WI: Schoenstatt Fathers, 1992), 169.

3. Beverly Roberts Gaventa, *Mary: Glimpses of the Mother of Jesus* (Minneapolis: Fortress Press, 1999), 64–66.

4. Alphonsus Liguori, *The Glories of Mary*, ed. Eugene Grimm (Brooklyn: Redemptorist Fathers, 1931), 392.

7. The Fleeing Mother

1. "Distance from Bethlehem to Alexandria," Timeanddate.com, accessed June 29, 2012: http://www.timeanddate.com/worldclock/distanceresult.html%3Fp1=1048&p2=426.

2. "On the Road," ChristianHistory.net, accessed August 20, 2012: http://www.christianitytoday.com/ch/1998/issue59/59h028.html.

3. *Catechism of the Catholic Church* (New York: Doubleday, 1995), 530.

4. *Catholic Encyclopedia*, newadvent.org, accessed August 20, 2012: http://www.newadvent.org/cathen/07419a.htm.

5. John Paul II, "Mass in the Indoor Stadium of Cairo," February 20, 2000, http://www.vatican.va/holy_father/

john_paul_ii/travels/documents/hf_jp-ii_hom_20000225_
cairo_en.html.

8. The Attentive Mother

1. "Contemplating the Wedding Feast of Cana," Creigh-
ton Online Ministries, accessed August 20, 2012, http://on-
lineministries.creighton.edu/CollaborativeMinistry/Imagi-
nation/cp-cana.html.

2. Brown, et al., *Mary in the New Testament*, 188–89.

3. Ibid., 189.

4. Ibid., 191.

5. Ibid., 192.

6. Ibid., 193.

9. The Grieving Mother-Child

1. Anne Catherine Emmerich, *The Dolorous Passion of Our
Lord Jesus Christ*, as recorded in the journal of Clement Bren-
tano, ed. Very Rev. C. E. Schmoger, C.SS.R., accessed July 7,
2012, http://www.jesus-passion.com/DOLOROUS_PAS-
SION_OF_OUR_LORD_JESUS_CHRIST.htm.

2. Marge Fenelon, *Ecce Mater Tua–Behold, Your Mother:
Marian Stations of the Cross* (Milwaukee: Icon Press, 2006), 25.

3. *Catechism of the Catholic Church*, 968.

4. John Paul II, *Salvifici Doloris*, February 11, 1984,
http://www.vatican.va/holy_father/john_paul_ii/apost_
letters/documents/hf_jp-ii_apl_11021984_salvifici-doloris_
en.html.

10. The Disciple Mother

1. *"Novena to the Spirit for the Seven Gifts,"* http://www.
ewtn.com/devotionals/pentecost/seven.htm.

2. *Catechism of the Catholic Church*, 726.

3. Ibid., 965.

4. Brown, et al., *Mary in the New Testament*, 235.

Conclusion

1. *Collection of Masses of the Blessed Virgin Mary, Volume 1* (New York: Catholic Book Publishing Co., 1992), 240.

2. Leo XIII, *Octobri Mense*.

3. Liguori, *The Glories of Mary*, 37.

4. *Catechism of the Catholic Church*, 721.

5. Ibid., 1641.

6. Kentenich, *Mary, Our Mother and Educator*, 95.

Marge Fenelon has been writing for Catholic and secular publications for nearly two decades. More than fifteen years ago, she decided to leave behind the secular business world in order to focus her talents and energies on serving the Church and Catholic media. She is a longtime contributor to a variety of Catholic and secular publications, including *Our Sunday Visitor* and *National Catholic Register*. Fenelon is also a contributor to *Catholic Lane, Integrated Catholic Life, CatholicMom.com*, and *Catholic Exchange*. Her column, "The Whirl," appears in the *Milwaukee Catholic Herald* and has won favorable reviews from laity and clergy alike. She is the author of several books related to Marian devotion and Catholic family life.

Fenelon is a regular guest on EWTN's *SonRise Morning Show* and has appeared on many others, including *Conversation with Cardinal Dolan*, Relevant Radio's *Morning Air*, and Spirit Catholic Radio's *Inside the Pages*. She is an enthusiastic speaker, and has invigorated audiences in a variety of venues. She holds a bachelor's degree in mass communications from the University of Wisconsin-Milwaukee and a certificate in spiritual mentoring from Cardinal Stritch University. Fenelon also holds a certificate in Marian studies from the International Marian Research Institute and is a member of the Mariological Society of America. She lives in Milwaukee.

Founded in 1865, Ave Maria Press,
a ministry of the Congregation of
Holy Cross, is a Catholic publishing
company that serves the spiritual and
formative needs of the Church and its
schools, institutions, and ministers;
Christian individuals and families; and
others seeking spiritual nourishment.

For a complete listing of titles from

Ave Maria Press

Sorin Books

Forest of Peace

Christian Classics

visit www.avemariapress.com

ave maria press® / Notre Dame, IN 46556
A Ministry of the United States Province of Holy Cross